TYPE 1,
Year One

TYPE 1, *Year One*

A MOTHER'S JOURNEY TO SUCCESSFULLY DECIPHER TYPE 1 DIABETES FOR HER NEWLY DIAGNOSED TEENAGER

MICHELE SEGURA

Type 1, Year One © Copyright 2023, Michele Segura

All rights reserved. No part of this publication may be reproduced, distributed or transmitted in any form or by any means, including photocopying, recording, or other electronic or mechanical methods, without the prior written permission of the publisher, except in the case of brief quotations embodied in critical reviews and certain other noncommercial uses permitted by copyright law.

The author and publisher do not assume and hereby disclaim any liability to any party for any loss, damage, or disruption caused by errors or omissions, whether such errors or omissions result from negligence, accident, or any other cause.

Adherence to all applicable laws and regulations, including international, federal, state and local governing professional licensing, business practices, advertising, and all other aspects of doing business in the US, Canada or any other jurisdiction is the sole responsibility of the reader and consumer.

Neither the author nor the publisher assumes any responsibility or liability whatsoever on behalf of the consumer or reader of this material. Any perceived slight of any individual or organization is purely unintentional. No compensation was received by any brand to be included in this book.

The opinions shared in the book reflect the personal research and experiences of the author and are not intended to substitute care from a trained healthcare provider or instructions from technology user manuals. Neither the author nor the publisher can be held responsible for the use of the information provided within this book. Please always consult a trained healthcare professional before making any decision regarding treatment for yourself or others.

ISBN: 979-8-89316-483-1 - ebook
ISBN: 979-8-89316-484-8 - paperback

DEDICATION

To the caregivers of type 1 warriors who want to make the right decisions but have no idea where to begin...

To the newly diagnosed young adults who want to have active, healthy lives...

To those who want to better understand the complexity of type 1 diabetes so they can support someone living with this autoimmune disease...

I see you.

This is Jonathan, one month before his type 1 diabetes (T1D) diagnosis and one year later. I am thankful for his willingness to share our journey through the first year of his diagnosis and the obstacles we overcame along the way, so that others recently diagnosed know that it is possible to live full and active lives with T1D.

CONTENTS

Introduction ix
Welcome To The T1d Club 1
Becoming A T1d Warrior 15
The Journey Is Personal 26
I'll Take A Side Of Insulin With That 44
Below The Carb Surface 65
It Isn't Stacking If Your Body Needs It 77
Staying Active 85
The Demons Of Highs And Lows 95
Technology: Dealing With Pricks,
    Pumps And Monitors 105
School And Work Accommodations 125
Creating A T1d Zone 143
Our Constant Travel Companion 148
Reconfirming Your Numbers Over Time 160
Finding Your Village 164
Contributing To The Cure 178
Diabetes Does Not Define Him 185
Type 1, Year One Takeaways 190
Resources 193
Acknowledgments 195
Author Bio 197

INTRODUCTION

I've walked a mile in the same shoes you are putting on right now. At the start of our type 1 diabetes (T1D) journey, it was hard to see any clear trail markers from the hospital room where my teenage son was recovering from diabetic ketoacidosis (DKA). I did not know which path would return us back to a normal life, but I was willing to explore them all in hopes of finding it.

Fear is the most crippling four-letter word I know. It stops people in their tracks and denies them the achievable goals that are most often just slightly beyond reach. If they would only take that one step forward, the goal would seem so much more attainable. Just one step. Just one decision. But when faced with an unfamiliar situation, one's innate desire to take the right step, to make the right decision becomes clouded. And that is how fear causes most people to freeze. Because they don't want to make the wrong decision. They don't want to be like the characters in horror movies – blindly run into the dense woods, the rickety abandoned house or the massive cornfield vs jumping in the fully-functioning vehicle and driving to safety. So, they do nothing. They dwell on the path where they encountered fear and fail to reach their destinations, their goals, their desired lives.

As I started our journey, I noticed that down every path I explored, there were people with type 1 diabetes who had been there for months, years, decades. They had discovered just enough to function well enough and didn't venture any further. And, in their minds, why should they? They were managing their diabetes according to what they were told by their doctors ... even though the strategies weren't keeping them in healthy glucose ranges. They were achieving the guidelines recommended by top diabetic health organizations ... even though following them meant they weren't as healthy as non-diabetic individuals. They were there because no one suggested to them that there are better paths to travel or ones that complement the paths they were already on – ones that allowed active lifestyles, normal health, and the ability to achieve their life goals.

I understand this.

There is a lot of T1D information available – but that doesn't mean it is easy to find, easy to understand and easy to determine how you can use it to live your best life. The guidance sometimes conflicts between sources. It can be vague. Often even dated. If you don't enjoy research or if rabbit holes make you weary it can be hard to condense all the guidance that is out there into something that can be easily consumed and digested. To make the gray, black and white.

For decades I have brought to life companies' missions, visions and strategic plans to positively impact members, employees and stakeholders. I have created and connected the dots in ways that enable others to understand ambiguous concepts and operationalize them into reality. I have not only made what's gray, black and white for others, but have added color so it is more attractive, appealing and memorable. I have done this for corporations, nonprofits and private businesses of all sizes. So, when presented with my son's T1D diagnosis, I took that same approach to understand how to best manage this disease.

This book does not focus on the disease, finding a cure, or discussing the different types of medications and treatments available. I am not a doctor and do not have medical training beyond general first aid. I knew very little about T1D and had limited first-hand experience with it prior to Jonathan's diagnosis. However, Jonathan's endocrinologist was so impressed with how we were managing his T1D, that she suggested I write a book to help others who were newly diagnosed. So, I did.

This book is a consolidation of how I used the extensive research I conducted during the first year of my teenager's type 1 diagnosis to get to a place where we were living with T1D – not just surviving. I share how we navigated what we learned to develop strategies that work for us. My hope is that it gives you a map of the available paths you can take to get to a life where diabetes management is in the background of your life.

Welcome to the Club shares Jonathan's diagnosis day and how I struggled to find clear answers for how to manage his T1D, which is what led me to write this book.

Becoming a T1D Warrior discusses the path to awareness and education, as well as how to handle the grief that accompanies being diagnosed as a teenager or young adult.

The Journey is Personal details how we determined Jonathan's basal and bolus strategies based on how his body responds to insulin, as well as how we approach treating low glucose levels.

I'll Take a Side of Insulin with That summarizes the importance of pre- and extended boluses, as well as the strategies we use when eating out, water consumption and supplements.

Below the Carb Surface outlines the many factors that impact insulin sensitivity and should be considered in addition to the carbohydrates that consume most of the T1D spotlight.

It isn't Stacking if Your Body Needs It examines the difference between stacking insulin and giving insulin corrections to help your body stay in a healthy glucose range.

Staying Active reviews how Jonathan approaches managing his T1D to be able to do all the things a young adult wants to do and should be able to do.

The Demons of Highs and Lows discusses the importance of staying in a tighter range than what is medically recommended because of how glucose levels outside of that range intrude on daily activities.

Technology: Dealing with Pricks, Pumps and Monitors describes the benefits of using current technology along with some ways to mitigate technology issues.

School and Work Accommodations outlines the steps we took to get Jonathan the accommodations he needs to be successful in high school, college and work.

Creating a T1D Zone talks through what we have done to ensure Jonathan can be more successful in managing his T1D supplies and how we have planned for emergencies.

Our Constant Travel Companion provides an overview of how we handle traveling and the tips we have found to make it less stressful.

Reconfirming Your Numbers Over Time shows the strategy used most often to validate personal basal, bolus and correction factors after health and lifestyle changes.

Finding Your Village covers how to get the most from your doctors, health insurance and support groups.

Contributing to the Cure shares Jonathan's participation in T1D research and why it is important to help in advancing treatment solutions and finding a cure.

Diabetes Does Not Define Him reminds us that we are more than our T1D diagnosis and, when successful in our diabetes management, we can focus on achieving our dreams.

If some of this terminology sounds foreign now, you will have a better understanding of it as you read this book. Most of it was foreign to me, too, at the beginning. Also, you can skip around the chapters and still have a full understanding of what is explained within each of them.

I originally intended this book to be a guide for new caregivers and young adults recently diagnosed with T1D – to assist them in being fearless in their approach to managing T1D. But through the drafting of this book, I realized friends and family can find it a valuable source to better understand the disease and how it affects their loved ones who have it and those who care for them. I also interviewed Jonathan and included his point of view to help those newly diagnosed know they are not alone in how they feel and think as they create their new normal.

May you find comfort in these worn soles. May we someday meet along our paths.

WELCOME TO THE T1D CLUB

MICHELE

I knew something was up. Jonathan was losing weight. I chalked it up to the intensity of carrying the tenor drums in the high school marching band performances, after-school practices and long days in general – all while masked due to the COVID mandates. He was a junior in high school and our district had returned to in-person classes for the 2020-21 school year. Jonathan was the percussion and drumline captain, in various school clubs and spent the little free time he had working on assignments for the NASA High School Aerospace online program as he wanted to be part of the team who explores Mars.

He was more tired than usual.
He was always hungry.
And he drank water like a fish.

Overall, he seemed fine. His annually school-required physical in August suggested he was boringly normal with no health concerns. He was growing and stretching out, I told myself. But I knew something was off. My momma senses were on high alert.

Winter break came and went. Marching season ended and his schedule wasn't as grueling. He was still the same. We talked.
"I think I want to see a doctor. Will you take me?"
It was Saturday.
"Of course. Do you want to go to the urgent care now or wait until Monday when I can get an appointment with your doctor?"
"I can wait."
So, we did.

January 25, 2021, is a day I will always remember. We sat in our vehicle outside our primary care doctor's office waiting for our appointment on that sunny Monday afternoon. The air was cool and crisp. We had our windows open to offset the sun's warm rays. Most doctor offices were still closed to in-office appointments. People were afraid. Doctors and nurses visited patients by their vehicles to minimize exposure to the COVID virus.

We were scheduled at 3 pm and it was now close to 5 pm. We chatted, laughed at memes, and found a way to put our concerns in the background. The cars around us slowly departed and it looked like our turn would be soon.

Our family doctor, dressed in hazmat scrubs, approached the passenger side of the car to talk with us. Jonathan explained his symptoms and concerns to his doctor of ten years who we barely recognize through all the protective wear.

"It doesn't sound like COVID. Come with me into the office."

We followed the doctor up the ramp, through the side door and into a small examination room. The office was quiet and dark. Most of the staff had already left for the day. He ran a few tests, took a blood sample and left the room.

We waited.
"Why do you think it is taking so long?"
"I don't know, but everything is going to be okay. Don't worry."
I tried to remain calm in front of Jonathan, but I was a nervous wreck inside. I've been in enough doctor offices to know the delay signaled something was up. The minutes ticked by slowly. There was nothing more on my phone to distract my thoughts.

Finally, close to 6 pm, his doctor came back into the room.
"I think Jonathan has had an onset of type 1 diabetes. His glucose is 363 and his A1C is 11."

"Wait. What?"
In my mind it didn't make sense. He was active. He was healthy. His choice of foods was great – no sodas, minimal junk food, lots of veggies and lean protein. I ate somewhat keto so, for the most part, my family did too.

"You need to go to the children's hospital in the San Antonio medical center right away. Jonathan is in diabetic ketoacidosis (DKA). Go to the emergency room. I will fax my findings over. They will be waiting for you." instructed our doctor.
"Are you sure?" I pressed. He was sure.

We listened. We asked questions.
There were no answers.
There is no cure.

"It will be fine. Think of it as an inconvenience, but your life will go on as normal," our doctor tried to reassure us. "You will just need to give yourself some insulin before each meal. One of my patients is an eighty-three-year-old farmer who has been a type 1 diabetic his whole life. No issues or complications. You will be fine. Let me get some paperwork for you before you go."

And our doctor left the room. Left us alone with this newfound life-changing diagnosis – which I would later understand this experience to be the norm for so many who had received the same news before us.

I took a deep breath. I called my husband. I stumbled to answer Jonathan's questions. We had no history on either side of the family. This had to be a mistake. I did not know enough about this autoimmune disease that had invaded our lives without a warning. His doctor came back into the room, handed us some paperwork, and said to follow up with him in two weeks.

We exited the doctor's office through that same side door, but into a different world.
"Am I going to die?" Jonathan asked, looking to me for the answers I did not have.
"Not today you're not. And not anytime soon. We will sort this out. You are going to be fine and feel a lot better once we get a handle on this. Give me a couple of days to get

up to speed on the information that is out there." I gave him a long hug.

He smiled at me in a way I knew he believed me. I had not let him down before. I would not let him down this time. We drove to the ER and checked in.

It was a long four days. Because of COVID, I was not allowed to leave the hospital room, and no one was allowed to visit. My husband, Alfredo, dropped off some clothes and other things for us at the hospital admissions desk and a nurse went down to retrieve them. It was like being on vacation but stuck in a tiny motel room because it was pouring rain outside. In reality, the sun was shining outside our hospital windows and doing its best to offer warmth and happiness to those who sought its friendly rays. It just couldn't penetrate through the walls and clouds that hung heavy in our hospital room.

Inside played out like a bad sci-fi movie. COVID protocol required the nurses to wear hazmat suits in the room. Their gear consisted of hair covers, masks and see-through visors, full-body protective gowns, gloves, shoe covers, the works. We never saw more than their eyes. They were cheery and professional as they collected blood, hung IV bags, connected Jonathan to various medical equipment and ran the tests they needed. The protective gear made it hard to understand them and hear the explanations they gave us for what they were doing. But we listened the best we could.

The pediatric endocrinologist visited with us via skype on the iPad that I, fortunately, had asked Alfredo to bring. Even then, she was wearing a mask because she was right outside the room and had to follow hospital protocol. She checked in on us daily. I liked her right away. She was knowledgeable and down-to-earth.

"I've got five other teenagers in here all recently diagnosed too. You did well to catch this as early as you did. Two high school athletes are in the ICU with numbers twice as high as yours." our new doctor told us. "We've seen a significant uptick in teenagers in the last few years. This really isn't a childhood disease anymore."

"There is a great amount of progress to find a cure and I am sure there will be one in Jonathan's lifetime," she tried to comfort us. "The technology available is really making a difference for those living with type 1. Right now, you can be anything you want, well, except an astronaut. Do you know what career you want to pursue, Jonathan?"

Jonathan hesitated. I held my breath. "I wanted to be an astronaut and travel to Mars. I'm part of a year-long NASA program for high school students."

Our doctor paused. "Well, who knows. Maybe you can still become one. Let's not give up hope just yet." I turned my head to wipe away the silent tear that snuck out of my eye. Honestly, the thought of having him leave this planet to venture into the unknown was not high on my list of what I hoped he would do, but the idea that it was no longer his decision to make pained me.

A few hours later, the hospital diabetes educator came in and gave me a stack of literature about eight inches high from various sources. "Read this," she said. "It explains everything and then we can discuss any questions you have."

She showed us how to check Jonathan's glucose with a glucose meter and finger prick and how to give insulin (called a bolus) for meals. She explained the importance of using the smaller, thinner needles so that they didn't hurt as much or leave marks. She demonstrated how to fill the syringe with insulin and ensure the bubbles were gone before injecting the precious fluid into the eight preferred areas on the body. She asked Jonathan if he wanted to administer the shots. He didn't. They had me give him the shots so that I would be comfortable doing it when we left the hospital.

I handled updating everyone in our circle of friends and family via texts and phone calls. My boss was great – she cleared my calendar and checked in with me daily. The school and teachers were supportive. Zachery, my older son, and Jonathan have an amazingly close relationship even though they are almost seven years apart. Zach checked on Jon regularly and lifted his spirits in a way only a brother can.

Jonathan took it all in stride. I was amazed at his resilience as we were overloaded with information on a constant basis. I knew the wheels were turning in his head, wondering what this new version of his life would be like. But that was a conversation for another day.

We played games and watched movies and then, when he slept, I poured through the pile of brochures and literature in the welcome packet determined to become an expert of this autoimmune disease, commonly referred to as T1D, overnight. What you don't know about me is that I am a nerd, an information junky, a type A momma with a master's degree in communications and English. I thrive on solving problems and I consume information like fresh baked chocolate chip cookies – you know the kind that are crunchy on the outside and chewy on the inside with loads of chocolate chips in every bite. And I have spent the last twenty years building strategies and culture stories for top Fortune 100 companies. So, after reading every page of the type 1 diabetes information provided to us as a newly diagnosed patient, it became brutally clear to me that this was going to be a personal journey where there are few standard answers.

The guidance was inconsistent as to when and how to bolus, what to eat, and how to live. The information from the American Diabetes Association said one thing while the Juvenile Diabetes Research Foundation recommended a slightly different approach. The tone was general and happy, but the Pink Panther mascot in the literature didn't make it any better. What kid even knows who the Pink Panther is anyways? The information seemed dated and was tailored toward young children. It left me with more questions than when I started.

I turned to the internet and read everything I could find online from reputable sources. I signed up for T1D Facebook support groups and podcasts and ordered some frequently mentioned books from Amazon that were waiting for me when I got home (*Sugar Surfing* by Dr. Ponder, *Think like a Pancreas* by Gary Scheiner, *Bright Spots and Landmines* by Adam Brown, and *Dr. Bernstein's Diabetes Solution*), and I made a list of running questions that I asked every time the doctor or diabetes educator stopped by.

When I pointed out the discrepancies in the provided information, the staff seemed surprised enough to make me think I was the first person who ever read it all. I also noticed that what was happening in the room was not what was suggested in any of the literature. The nurses were generally caring, but it was clear they hadn't had much in the way of type 1 diabetes training. For example, the literature said to bolus for the number of carbs and then eat. However, the nurses would drop off Jonathan's food and then leave without providing his insulin. Sometimes it would be more than an hour before they returned with insulin in hand to help us calculate how many units to bolus. By this time, the finger prick showed he had climbed back into the 300s since his food was already digesting in his stomach. When I questioned this, I was told they wanted to ensure they knew how many carbs he ate before they calculated the insulin for his meals so he wouldn't get too much. I thought to myself, "He is in DKA. At this point, I don't think you can give him too much insulin for his meals based on whether or not he ate everything."

Also, his meals always included about fifty to sixty grams of simple carbs and were items like mashed white potatoes, yeast rolls, whole milk, and canned fruit options. This wasn't how we ate at home, and it didn't seem like what he should be eating in the hospital since these items normally spike a person's glucose. Even with my lack of expertise,

I knew these meals were not optimal to managing this disease.

I let our new doctor know what was happening and she agreed he should be getting the insulin prior to eating – and would pass along the needed training. She also put in the order to get insulin with the meal. Going forward, we did bolus before he ate, but we still didn't know how important it was to pre-bolus and wait for the insulin to start working before eating.

And then, just like that. For no real clear reason to us, it was determined that Jonathan was stable enough and we knew enough about managing T1D to be on our own. We were being discharged.

As we left the hospital, it felt like I was walking out as a first-time mom who had no idea what to do with a newborn – only this was my second child, and he was a teenager. I don't know how else to describe it. This beautiful boy next to me had lived one life for the past sixteen years and now needed to learn a completely different one. I had prescriptions for long-acting insulin pens, short-acting insulin pens, needles, blood test strips, glucagon, and a glucose meter. I had a well-worn copied paper of a glucose sliding scale for boluses, a diary to keep track of how much we bolused and when, and a follow-up appointment to meet with the pediatric endocrinologist who would guide us on this less than magical journey. I also had a twenty-four hour emergency number to call in case I had questions. It all looked so simple on paper. But our bodies are too complex for me to believe it was going to be this easy.

What I didn't have were simple answers and an understanding as to how to make this work for Jonathan. All I knew was that it was now up to me to save my son's life every day until he was educated enough to save it himself – and then I would still be there if he needed me.

JONATHAN

Before I was diagnosed, I didn't feel good, but I didn't realize how bad I really felt.

I was working out in the gym to get fit, stronger, and gain a few pounds of muscle. However, instead of gaining weight, I was losing it. I went from my standard frame of about 145 pounds to a measly 130 pounds before I was diagnosed and put in the hospital. By the time I left the hospital to begin my road to recovery, I was down to 128 pounds.

I was always tired and my heart seemed to be racing on a normal basis. I never felt good after a meal. I thought it was because I must not be eating as well as I should. The most annoying thing is that I began to have to pee more than normal. I would get up three to four times a night and then still have to make multiple pit stops throughout the day. I wasn't sure what was going on, but I asked my mom to take me to the doctor.

When my primary doctor told my mom and me the news, I didn't know what T1D was. But seeing him struggling with the right words as he told us and watching my mother's reaction, I couldn't help but feel my life was about to be turned around – and little did I know by how much.

I was happy that we went to the doctor when we did because he was able to diagnose me before my blood sugar became dangerously high. For those who haven't had to experience being told you have T1D, when you are diagnosed you more than likely will have to go to the hospital immediately because your body is, in effect, dying since it is unable to convert the food you are putting into your body into energy.

Even though it was now apparent that my body had been fighting the onset of T1D for a while, my active lifestyle, thankfully, kept the damage to my body to a minimum. In fact, the doctors told me when I was in the hospital that there were two other teenagers who were admitted with blood sugar levels above 700 mg/dL – which is more the norm for diagnosis than to be discovered in the 300s like what happened with me.

I know that T1D is not the worst thing in the world to be diagnosed with, but that doesn't mean it is easy to accept. The four days in the hospital felt like an eternity of sadness. Lying in my bed while multiple doctors came in numerous times to explain what this autoimmune disease meant for me. The thoughts that kept playing in my mind were:

"Why me?",
"Did I do something wrong?",
"How will I live a normal life?",
"What will people think of me?".

Then they told me that I would be the exact same person, I would just have to inject myself with insulin every time I ate. "Okay" I thought, "This doesn't sound too bad".

Getting out of the hospital was a magical moment for me. One thing they tell you is that you will start feeling really good when you get out of the hospital because you now have insulin in your body and your body has flushed out the ketones. And to my surprise, they were right! The best way to describe it is like the chains of Hell that were unknowingly binding and smothering me were lifted off by God himself. That may sound dramatic but T1D is a disease that, without treatment, eventually consumes the person it invades.

BECOMING A T1D WARRIOR

MICHELE

For most people, the diagnosis day we experienced is all too familiar. The raw emotions, the lack of understanding, the unfamiliar lingo, the feelings of isolation, the hospital stay, and the uncertainty of what tomorrow will bring. It hit us out of the blue and caused us to play the "what if" or "did I do something to cause this" game over and over in our heads.

Both our primary care doctor and our new endocrinologist had told us that the medical field still doesn't know what triggers or starts the autoimmune response that creates type 1 diabetes (T1D) in the body and that there is nothing we did to cause it. What they do know is that if you have the genetic markers, at some point in your life you will most likely develop T1D. Current treatments and research have been successful in delaying the onset for some people, but not preventing it.

As I became integrated in this community, learning more and hearing more about others' journeys, I realized more awareness is needed to help our society know that this autoimmune disorder can onset at any age if you are predisposed to developing it.

With the T1D diagnosis, your family becomes part of the elite warriors drafted to fight a lifelong war. When your teenager is frustrated or his glucose is out of whack, he will roll his eyes at you and tell you he is the one who must live with the disease every minute of every day. It is his body. They are his battles. But for most parents (and I know you are one because you are reading this book), it is now part of our lives as well. I would trade places with Jonathan in a heartbeat but must settle with fighting alongside him. It is a pain only a parent can experience.

I learned long ago for other reasons that having the will to win doesn't matter, it is the will to prepare that determines success. I recognized the best way to fight alongside him was to help him prepare for attack on all fronts (carbs aren't the only enemy). By educating ourselves on how to manage T1D, understanding and advocating for his rights, and taking advantage of all health insurance benefits – we have learned how to live somewhat peacefully with this invader.

Need for Awareness

Before Jonathan's diagnosis, I thought T1D was a childhood illness that we no longer had to worry about once our children entered elementary school. The few friends I know with T1D family members all developed T1D before the age of six. In fact, it used to be called juvenile diabetes because most diagnoses occurred in children. Even the materials given to us in the hospital and the additional research papers and studies that I read still mainly identified T1D as a childhood disease. There isn't enough general awareness and discussion around the fact that a good portion of T1D is now being diagnosed in people between the ages of fourteen and twenty-one with some onsets happening well into adulthood.

One of the things I did early on was to reach out to my trusted network of friends to help me find professionals with T1D who could talk with Jonathan and let him know that everything would be alright. We were lucky enough to speak with a couple of doctors, scientists (including one at NASA), and other professionals during the first six weeks of his diagnosis. Everyone was amazingly open and gave Jonathan such encouragement. They shared their stories, challenges and successes, and how they live with T1D. They all became T1D warriors between the ages of seventeen to twenty-two. Most were also patient zero in their family trees. They had similar diagnosis stories, and all remember feeling lost and unsure about how to move forward with their lives during those days and months after developing T1D.

When we did learn about the available genetic markers testing, Zachery, Jonathan's older brother, asked to be tested. His results came back negative for the markers that predispose him to developing T1D in his lifetime. It seems like these simple blood tests should be a standard part of infant and childhood pediatric visits. If they had been offered to us, we probably would have opted for the testing long ago for awareness purposes. To me, it makes sense. Locally, it helps families better prepare, if necessary, by giving them time to educate themselves on the disease, treatment options, and potential medication that could delay the onset as long as possible. And globally, it could help to advance treatment research and in finding a cure. Imagine how much available data goes uncollected because we aren't more proactive in learning about how, why, and when this disease is triggered and working with individuals before the onset happens.

Education

What is prevalent in society is a focus on type 2 diabetes. I think this is true because type 2 is often behavior driven and there are more opportunities to reverse it or put it in remission. Making changes to one's behaviors – increasing exercise and removing fatty food and sugars from one's diet – can keep a person from having to take medication to control the health issues associated with type 2. Some people opt for this lifestyle; many opt for a combination or go the full medication route. Regardless of the chosen path, the healthcare industry knows it can make a difference in these people's lives and they can demonstrate proven results. As humans we are drawn to situations where there are opportunities to overcome, to "win". And because there are all kinds of prescriptions and solutions to manage and control type 2, there are more commercials and marketing to drive patients to a particular drug, app, eating and/or exercise program, etc., thereby generating more awareness for the condition as well as paths that lead to healthier lives for those individuals.

Frequently when people hear "diabetes", they immediately say inappropriate comments and give incorrect advice. We heard this from the most well-meaning people. One family member asked Jonathan if he will graduate to type 2 when he turns eighteen. In her mind, she thought type 1 identified children who have diabetes and type 2 identified adults. Period. No real distinction between the two conditions other than age. Another person told Jonathan he must have eaten too many sweets when he was younger. Again, the individual was attributing type 2 causes to type 1 because all that person knows is what he sees in the media. And there is always the person who thinks type 1 can be reversed naturally and will send you various homeopathic remedies to try. This lack of general understanding and distinction between the two makes it harder to be a person managing T1D.

Type 2 diabetes is not an invader like T1D. It's more of a frenemy who is gradually allowed to coexist in one's life. What's not talked about is while T1D is most likely triggered by stress, illness (usually a virus), puberty, trauma, and/or other factors in those individuals who are predisposed to developing this autoimmune disorder, there is ultimately nothing the individual can do to stop this invasion. And often it is so hard to identify when exactly the pancreas began to malfunction. Depending on how active a person is and the diet one eats, it can take several months for the body to get to diabetic ketoacidosis (DKA) and to notice something isn't right. I mean the A1C number we all focus on in every endocrinologist appointment is a measurement of the average glucose levels over the past ninety days – so the majority of people aren't even alerted that something is wrong for at least two to three months after the onset.

And if the person is more active or eats a generally low carb diet, it may take even longer because the pancreas isn't working extra hard to eliminate large amounts of glucose in the body caused by food and lifestyle choices.

In the short time we have been part of this community, there has been an increase of mainstream media exposure around T1D – mostly from the Dexcom continuous glucose monitoring system (CGM) and the Omnipod 5 insulin pump marketing efforts. It has helped with awareness, but not really with education. The general public still doesn't understand that type 1 is an autoimmune disease where the body no longer creates insulin and type 2 is a condition where the body has become resistant to the insulin it produces. In conversations with our endocrinologist, we both agree the disease should be renamed and further distanced from type 2 diabetes to help distinguish between the two. Many in the T1D community also agree. Maybe the medical field should hold a renaming contest where only those who are affected by T1D can submit entries? I am sure there will be a few suggestions submitted.

Handling Grief

I'm not going to sugarcoat it. There are dark days for everyone during the first year, maybe longer. Jonathan was busy trying to fit in while doing things differently. We did the best we could to keep diabetes in the background when we were out and about or when he participated in school and group activities. We carried low carb buns with us to football games and marching contests so he could get a burger like everyone else without spiking so

Type 1, Year One

high that it affected his ability to perform. He sipped on regular Gatorade and ate protein bars to keep his glucose levels in range while playing basketball, during paintball competitions and throughout his workout routines. On the outside, he was crushing it. He continued to achieve straight As in his classes, made his friends laugh often, completed the NASA program as a finalist with a 99% grade, and memorized his music with perfection. His glucose reports showed he was in range more than 90% of the time and he was almost completely self-sufficient in his diabetic management.

On the inside, Jonathan wondered if it was all worth it. Did his life really matter anymore. He once shared with me the hard questions he mulled in his head, "What is the point of all of this when I need insulin to survive? My life is now in the hands of the makers of insulin and glucose technology. What if they decide to stop making it or there is a shortage, and we are unable to find it? What if they determine my life isn't necessary? What choices do I have?"

Sometimes strength comes from your darkest moments; from the times you chose to not give up. What choices did he have? Well, he had the choice to work through his emotions and come out on the side of fighting for the life he wants.

I recognized that he was going through the five stages of grief that is best explained by Elisabeth Kubler Ross and David Kessler. It is a concept I came across during a research paper I wrote in college. He had to grieve for the life he planned and accept that his new reality would be just as great. The five stages are denial, anger, bargaining, depression, and acceptance. Here he was at the height of his teenage years, on the cusp of adulthood and working toward his dream of space, when he was blindsided with a condition that, for now, meant his dream would be out of reach. Who doesn't need time to grieve in that situation?

I think this is the cruelty for those who have on onset of T1D as a teenager or young adult – they actually know another way of life. Diagnosed as a toddler or child has its own complications and issues. I have read the many struggles posted by these caregivers who are dealing with a baby who can't yet communicate, general growth and puberty issues, how to put technology on a tiny body and more. But for the most part, the toddler/child diagnosed with T1D doesn't remember life any other way. Newly diagnosed teens and young adults have to grieve their old lives before they can accept a new beginning.

And I had to allow Jonathan to do that. But not for too long. He didn't need to dwell in the grief, he needed to begin living this new life so he could find the joys and opportunities in it. We worked through the denial phase in those first few weeks with lots of compassionate, tough love. The rest of the phases seem to still be a cyclical journey. When I think we have worked our way to acceptance, something happens and we are back in the anger stage. Because even after a year, the diagnosis is still new, still raw. But we keep moving forward on our path one step at a time to move past the grief.

I do this by listening to him unconditionally and allowing him to express his emotions and concerns. This takes time and commitment. It is not something that can be done while multi-tasking and should not be attempted if your teen isn't in a good glucose range (the conversation will not be valuable because of the high/low glucose effects on the emotions and thought process – which I discuss later in the book). I have learned that if it isn't urgent, I need to wait to talk about a topic with Jonathan until he brings it up. Sometimes we go weeks without him wanting to talk about anything diabetes-related except bolusing for meals. And then, out of the blue, he tells me something that has been on his mind and he is ready to discuss my recommendations in detail.

I also keep him involved in what he loves so that he sees he can still do it all – just a little differently than the rest. This comes in the form of reassurance, encouragement, research, mentors and trainers, and trial and error of successful insulin management.

And through this process, he has become a warrior. Cliché as it may sound, as someone with T1D, he actually appreciates some of the accomplishments and successes more than before being diagnosed. He overcomes additional struggles, most of the time unnoticed, and for that he relishes in the successes more so. During one of our conversations, he told me he realized that people weren't going to judge him solely on having T1D, but they would view him on how he puts himself out there despite having T1D. He determined that he wants to show people what he was made of and not focus on what he was lacking.

JONATHAN

I hate diabetes.

And not just from the medical standpoint, but I hate the name too. If someone asked me to rate it, I would give it one star and not recommend it to anyone.

As someone who strives to be fit and active, I do not like telling people that I have type 1 diabetes because they don't understand it. They immediately assume that if I had eaten healthier and exercised more, I could have prevented this. This is because most everyone only knows diabetes from what they hear about type 2 on the television and in marketing materials.

Truthfully this is the reason why I struggled for so long to be okay with telling people.

Being diagnosed at sixteen was hard for me because I felt like my whole life was about to start. Then it was ripped away from me like some cruel joke.

I do miss my old life, before I was diagnosed.

Every day I ponder whether I will ever see that version of my life again. Will there ever be a cure that enables me to live without a CGM or insulin pump attached somewhere to my body? Will I ever be able to do anything and everything without worrying about how it might impact my blood sugar?

For people who were diagnosed as babies or very early as a child, they often don't remember life without T1D. Even if they have moments of anger and frustration with this autoimmune disease, they don't have to grieve for a life lost to it. I feel people who have had type 1 their entire lives do not understand my grief.

I read a quote once that has changed my perspective and reminds me that there is life beyond my temporary grief, but I must be willing to push through it: "God gave you this battle for a reason, now stand up and fight!"

And that is what I intend to do today and every day going forward. I told my mom I was okay with her writing this book in the hopes that my journey will help others. I still pray for a cure, but for now, I choose to live my best life with T1D.

THE JOURNEY IS PERSONAL

MICHELE

Being prepared does not require me to have all the answers. It means being able to find solutions in the midst of the chaos. Once we arrived home from the hospital, we took the next week to get familiar with the new routine and get Jonathan ready to go back to school. This included him being comfortable with giving himself insulin shots.

For the first few days, he wanted me to give both the long-acting and mealtime boluses. We talked about how to administer the shots. How to apply the needle to the pen and prime the needle. Then how to set the bolus amount of insulin and where it seemed to work best for him. Slowly he started to give them on his own. First, he had me set up the insulin pens and then he bolused. By the end of the week, he took the reins for the complete process; all I did was tell him how much to bolus.

I took time to educate myself as much as I could and explain everything to Jonathan, so we were on the same page with his care. This is important as a parent with a newly diagnosed teenager because:

- Jonathan needs to be included in his care decisions. I have less time with him before he is out on his own in this world. He was diagnosed midway through his junior year in high school and would be headed off to college within eighteen months.

- As a teenager, there are more opportunities to be in situations where I am not present, and he will make his own decisions. I want him to make educated ones – to include knowing how to correct his glucose level if needed.

- He must be able to advocate for himself and the best way to do this is to arm him with knowledge. This includes school and employment situations, as well as doctor appointments.

I've learned a lot about this autoimmune disease in a short time, but I don't consider myself an expert by any means. I know type 1 diabetes (T1D) will continue to teach us more throughout Jonathan's life. The human body is so complex that it would be a false sense of security to assume that we could gather enough knowledge of a bodily function/organ to know everything that could happen in a lifetime. I recognize that we will make mistakes, but success and mistakes go hand in hand. The difference is learning from those mistakes and keeping at it until we get it right.

Trust me, you will over bolus and under bolus. You will even forget to bolus at least once. Or twice. Probably more. That doesn't mean you messed up or that you are a horrible caregiver or person with T1D. I like to categorize these incidents more as research than mistakes. Trial and error. Our whole lives are just that, so being a T1D is simply another variation to test.

I have to give myself grace in these situations and remember that I am barely starting out. Our endocrinologist is impressed that Jonathan remains in the medically recommended glucose range more than 90% of the time this close to diagnosis so we must be doing something right.

Through educating myself on the material, research and guidance that is out there, I have determined that this is a personal journey of care. I also realize that this doesn't mean we are alone on this journey. There are others all walking similar paths toward healthier lives. Some have studied this disease much longer and have a firmer grasp on the fundamentals. There will always be a T1D veteran who posts amazingly straight glucose lines and seems to know exactly what to do in every situation. Don't let that frustrate your progress. They have had years of experience with their diabetes management. See their successes as goals to achieve. Learn from them and recognize that what you want to do is possible if you are willing to work at it.

But you must be willing to work at it.

You will have to do the work at some point. Either you do the work upfront and have more successes sooner. Or you struggle with stubborn highs and scary lows until you are tired and frustrated enough to take the time to understand how your body works and responds to insulin, activities and food. Ask any T1D veteran if this is true. They will tell you "Yes" and also openly provide support by sharing tips, tricks, carb counts, new bolusing concepts and so much more.

There really are many different ways to manage T1D based on your lifestyle and diet. Some of these concepts we have researched and decided we are not ready to experiment with because of our lifestyle or where Jonathan is in regard to the maturity of managing his T1D. And that is okay. We may consider using some of them eventually, but for now, those ideas are tucked away for another day. The important thing is to know there are alternative methods out there should we hit a plateau in his diabetes management or have a lifestyle change that could benefit from alternative strategies.

Determining Your North

Girl Scouts taught me that to be successful in any journey, I have to start with the right navigation and create a plan to get there. I knew the most important factor in setting Jonathan up for success was to get his personal numbers dialed in correctly.

Now if you knew me, you would understand that my goal early on was to get Jonathan into a healthy glucose range as soon as possible. I was thankful we caught his T1D onset earlier than what the doctors told us is normally seen. What I learned those first few weeks after he was diagnosed is that Jonathan didn't feel good when he was in normal range. When his glucose was around 100 mg/dL, he would have all the symptoms of a low and feel sick. It was too soon. No matter what I wanted, I would have to adjust to what Jonathan needed. His body had been functioning at the higher range for so long that his body considered that range as "normal" and would falsely signal him as being low. I had to step his glucose range down slowly.

I decided I would adjust his glucose levels over three weeks. Initially, my goal was to keep him between 140-200 mg/dL between meals. Then I targeted 100-150 mg/dL. Then to 80-150 mg/dL with a goal of getting him to 70-140 mg/dL which is the normal healthy glucose range for non-diabetic teenagers and adults.

That is something I noticed right away in my research that bothered me. There are always two separate ranges – one for those with diabetes and a different one for those without.

Healthy Blood Glucose Level Recommendations from the ADA*		
Time	Without Diabetes	With Diabetes
Fasting	70-99 mg/dL	80-130 mg/dL
1-2 hours after meals	< 140 mg/dL	< 180 mg/dL
A1C results	< 5.7%	< 7%

*as of January 2023

Why does the American Diabetes Association (ADA) recommend overall diabetic targets be from 80-180 mg/

dL while the ranges for people without diabetes are well under that?

It is even suggested that sleeping in the upper portion of that range is acceptable. Why? I understand the whole low glucose coma concerns that were drilled in our heads before we departed the hospital, but it doesn't account for the long-term medical effects that are caused by running constantly high or even the short-term effects of how the individual feels after sleeping at that high glucose level all night – which is crummy for Jonathan. Sleep is a chance for the body to heal, grow and rebalance. The body can't focus on those necessities if it is busy trying to remove excess glucose. Our nighttime goal is a nice steady line between 85-100 mg/dL. If he is higher than 140 mg/dL, he wakes up with a headache and feels completely exhausted regardless of the number of hours he slept. I imagine someone sleeping close to 180 mg/dL all night must feel even worse.

As for long-term effects, so what if the person doesn't experience those medical issues for decades, I am still setting up my son for failure if I let him stay in the higher ranges and don't teach him how to live targeting normal glucose ranges. I don't want him to have to worry about retinopathy, cataracts, glaucoma, kidney disease, neuropathy issues, strokes, cognitive impairments, coronary heart disease and lack of blood flow in his arms and legs – and these are only the complications reported most often. He has enough to worry about with T1D that I am not knowingly going to add these additional concerns to that list.

And so that is what we did. We stepped him down into normal glucose ranges over the next few weeks. This was accomplished through a combination of understanding his fast-acting insulin needs, his personal sliding scale, and his required long-acting insulin basal levels.

As you can guess, I called the after-hours emergency number a lot during those first thirty days to readjust his insulin strategy and find his personal range. Our endocrinologist was great and worked with me to make adjustments about every three to four days. She explained that Jonathan was honeymooning and we would most likely have to readjust his numbers once that ended – but it could take months or even years for that to happen. (*Honeymooning is the term used to describe the period after being diagnosed as a T1D where your remaining beta cells are still healthy enough to contribute in some fashion to your body's insulin needs.*)

Jonathan's glucose levels ran very low when he was sleeping to the point where we were sending him to bed with an uncovered protein shake and still waking him up a couple of times a night to get him above 70 mg/dL, so I knew he had too much insulin in his system. We started with 25 units of long-lasting insulin during a twenty-four hour period and after making several adjustments ended with 4 units. Figuring out the bolusing strategy was a bit trickier because it is similar to balancing scales. There is a relationship between the insulin-to-carb ratio, sliding scale and correction factor so when you make adjustments to one, it may impact the calculations for the others.

During our testing phase, Jonathan ate the same breakfast, lunch and snacks to help us decipher his personal numbers. After meals, it seemed Jonathan's glucose level stayed higher longer than it should. We tested and moved his insulin-to-carb ratios, eventually ending up with 1:10 in the mornings, 1:8 in the afternoons and 1:9 in the evenings. We even changed up his sliding scale several times as we moved him toward the lower glucose range before we landed on the right correction factor, which was correcting over 120 mg/dL with a ratio of 1:27 during the day, 1:28 in the evenings and 1:29 for late night snacking to help prevent unplanned low glucose levels while he slept. We achieved this by making detailed notes on his food, insulin, and activities and sharing them with his endocrinologist.

While the tracking chart we were given in the hospital was good, I wanted to collect more detail. For each meal I tracked the time, current glucose reading, number of carbs and units of insulin given in addition to notes such as if we were trying a new ratio or what he ate for dinner, if we had adjusted his long-acting insulin, if his continuous glucose monitor (CGM) captured a significant spike after the meal, and what activities he participated in that day.

We did this type of tracking while we were doing multiple daily injections (MDI) because it was easy to manage and I left it on the kitchen counter so I could reference it as needed. As we moved to the Dexcom CGM and Omnipod insulin pump, I started tracking his food through the SugarMate app because it gave us a better picture of what was happening and the data helped us to better refine what we were learning.

Another thing we tracked when he was MDI is where he gave himself insulin (bolusing). He tended to bleed in the arms so we decided to avoid that area after a few injections in those sites. His legs were already pretty muscular and we noted that an injection in his thigh was absorbed much quicker than anywhere else. In fact, I learned that injecting insulin into the muscle and then using that muscle group helps the insulin to be absorbed more rapidly. So that was our preferred site when we needed to get insulin in him quickly – inject in the thigh and then go for a short walk.

By our first follow up in March (about sixty days after being diagnosed), Jonathan's A1C was down to 6.9% and 90+% in range. By the summer he was down to 5.7% and has continued to keep his A1C in the normal, non-diabetic glucose range ever since. More importantly, he also continues to maintain a 90+% time in range which means we are not achieving the lower A1C level at the expense of significant rollercoaster glucose levels.

Finding Your Personal Fifteen

Anyone who has been introduced to T1D recognizes the number 15. It seems to be the number that is used for general guidance:

- We started with a 1:15 insulin-to-carb ratio for food
- We are told any food under 15 carbs is a free food and doesn't require insulin
- If running low, consume 15 carbs and wait 15 minutes before repeating until you are back in range

I thought this was true for the first few weeks. But it's not. At least not for us. As I mentioned earlier, through eating the same thing every day we learned that he actually needed three different insulin-to-carb ratios for most days – and none of them involved the number fifteen. After much trial and error, we learned that Jonathan needed the most insulin in the morning, less in the afternoons and an average between the two for the evenings. When we moved to the Omnipod insulin pump, we were able to adjust his basal settings to account for the variations in his day so that the insulin-to-carb ratios worked the majority of the time.

We also learned that there are really no free fifteen carb foods (unless we are catching a low or he has completed a recent workout). Most everything impacts his glucose – some take longer to show, so it wasn't as easy to associate the rise with the culprit right away without keeping a journal, wearing a continuous glucose monitor (CGM), and tracking it through the Sugarmate app. Even snacks that have less than five carbs add up to more than fifteen uncovered carbs over time if left untreated. We did determine that a serving or two of plain, raw veggies doesn't impact him – but as a growing and active teenage boy, he rarely wants to eat just that. Go figure.

Now that he has the Omnipod 5 insulin pump, Jonathan is able to get away with a nibble here or there or a small protein snack without bolusing because the pump adjusts as his glucose rises. We don't make this a habit, but it is nice to know that if we are off a few carbs in the calculation, his pump covers for us.

Regarding giving Jonathan fifteen carbs for a low, that is way too much – at least for now. The first couple of times we did this, he shot up almost 100 points. And then we had to calm the rollercoaster effect. After trying all the recommendations we read about (such as Skittles, Sweet Tarts, gummy bears, jellybeans, Life Savers, mints, Starbursts, marshmallows, juice boxes, and honey) to treat a low, Jonathan settled on straight glucose tablets for the majority of the time and Transcend glucose gel packets if he is in the middle of an activity.

He never was a big candy or sweets kid growing up. Most of the time when he was younger, I would take his Trick-or-Treat score from Halloween into the office by the following week because he was done eating it. Jonathan would also ask me to make all kinds of homemade desserts and then forget about them after a day or two, resulting in me sending them off to work with my husband so I wasn't tempted to finish them on my own.

I ordered a couple sets of the glucose tablet ten count tubes off of Amazon and put in monthly subscriptions for the larger refill bottles and big bags of Transcend glucose gel packets. There is a tablet tube in each of our vehicles, by his bed, in his bathroom, in the kitchen, in his backpack, by his drum set, on his desk, by his gaming computer, in his workout bag and in my purse. You get the picture. You can also find the Transcend packets in his backpack, crossbody sling and workout bag.

Every Sunday, I walk through the house and refill all the tablet tubes. It gives me an idea as to how he is self-managing without having to ask. I learn a lot from how many tablets are left in each tube. Is he treating lows in the wee hours of the night? Does he have too much insulin on board when he is walking around campus? Does he need to re-evaluate how he is preparing for his workouts to prevent extreme lows? Sometimes I even find two or three tubes in one location or empty tubes where I stash the extra supplies. This helps me in navigating his needs, the pump algorithms and how I continue to educate us both on better insulin management strategies.

Each of his glucose tablets is four carbs. If we are chasing a steadily declining low, he starts with one to see how he reacts before eating another one. If he is already low or if the Dexcom arrow is trending down, he might eat two of them right away and then we watch and repeat as necessary. Two important thoughts we keep in mind:

- Verify the number with a finger prick. We have made the mistake of treating a low based on the CGM reading only to discover by finger prick that it wasn't really that low after all.
- Patience is a must in these situations. Too many carbs too fast cause a glucose rebound is often harder to treat.

If Jonathan starts to feel low while he is in class or performing, he immediately treats the low and may follow up with a protein bar that has about ten carbs in it. We do this with peanut butter crackers and protein shakes as well. Once he starts heading back up, he boluses for some portion of the carbs he consumed depending on how he is trending. Sometimes he won't need to do anything because his glucose has leveled off in the range he wants. For us, we first treat the low with a simple carb so that it can be quickly absorbed before adding a protein to help balance the levels longer term.

When Jonathan moved to the Omnipod 5, we had to re-evaluate how he treated his lows. If he catches the low before the pump stops insulin delivery, then he treats it the same. However, if the pump has stopped administering insulin, he may need less carbs to treat the low, because he also has less insulin entering his body. Checking to see how long the pump has stopped delivering insulin is a good strategy to use to determine how many carbs you may need to treat the low and avoid going too high.

Through trial and error, we have learned that we don't need to hop on the proverbial rollercoaster to treat a low – I like to say, "let's keep the rollercoasters in the amusement parks and out of our glucose levels". With patience and knowledge, we can redirect and steadily get him back into his desired range.

We do have juice boxes and many of the other options available, which has come in handy when his glucose level unexpectedly drops into the urgent low levels (50s and below). This has happened a handful of times, even after we had deciphered his insulin needs. Maybe it was the time he forgot to calibrate his Dexcom only to feel low at 80 mg/dL and learn that he was actually at 56 mg/dL. Or maybe it was that time he came home from an extra-long leg day workout and the insulin he bolused for his meal went right through the food and dropped him into the 40s. Or maybe it was the time during our vacation when

Type 1, Year One

we ate a big dinner and then walked along the beach, only to have the cardio effect kick in quicker than usual and realize the Dexcom is showing 64 mg/dL with a straight arrow down. While Jonathan enjoyed his brother giving him a piggyback ride to the condo to slow the rate of the glucose drop, the unexpected fall with nothing on hand was terrifying. Whatever the reason, we now have simple carbs around us at all times to aid him as needed.

A few things we did learn during our trial-and-error phase is that treating a low is definitely a time when all carbs are not created equal. To treat a low, we stay with simple dextrose options. Most people with T1D agree that chocolate, ice cream, cookies and crackers aren't good carb sources for treating lows. The fat in these items delays the glucose from rising quickly. This results in overcorrecting, forcing you to treat a high later.

Also, not all juice boxes are created equal. They come in a variety of carb counts. I have seen them as low as eight carbs per box and as high as thirty carbs per box. It is important to get the right type of juice box that works best for your personal needs.

With the current supply shortages, we sometimes have issues finding the juice boxes we want, so I ordered small 4 oz plastic bottles on Amazon that we refill with Jonathan's favorite all natural juice to keep the refrigerator stocked. I also avoid having to measure things during an urgent low. Sometimes it is crazy enough just trying to get the glucose back into range that we don't want to worry about calculating the carbs we are consuming. Others appear to be great at this, but it doesn't work for us.

JONATHAN

When I came home from the hospital, I didn't really know what to do. I did know, however, that my mom would make it her mission to figure it all out. That is the way she is about most things. She did a lot of research and shared with me what she learned and how she thought it would apply to me. She didn't hesitate to call the doctor's emergency number those first few weeks when she had questions and make recommendations to the doctors as to how to adjust my ratios. I am always thankful for her, even though sometimes she bombards me with new information on a regular basis.

Honestly, in those first few months I was still trying to accept what was now my life.

I should also tell you that I was the kid who ran from needles in the doctor's office. Just to give you some perspective, in middle school we had a student test positive for tuberculosis and every student who had any potential contact with said student, had to go through two rounds of blood testing months apart. It was a big deal even though no one else tested positive. The Texas department of Health Services set up our school gymnasium both times to look like a disaster response area. When it was my day to draw blood, my mom would come to school to look after me because I experienced a vasovagal reaction and would have to lay down during the process so I didn't faint.

Now, I have a lifetime of pricking my fingers, giving myself shots, attaching technology under my skin, and having quarterly blood tests – the irony doesn't escape me. So for the first few days after my diagnosis, I let my mom administer the insulin to help me overcome my aversion to needles. The pens helped out quite a bit with this because the needle is so small. After that, I was pretty comfortable bolusing on my own.

I am a creature of habit, so when my mom wanted me to eat the same meals to understand how my body reacts to insulin, I was fine with it. I am glad my mom did this because waking up every night to treat the lows was impacting my days. School work, band, and hanging out with friends is tough when combined with ongoing sleepless nights. The adjustments also helped me get back into the gym faster. This process made me realize early on that I had to learn what worked best for me; and that gave me confidence later to take more control of my insulin management.

Figuring out how to deal with lows early in my diagnosis was a struggle because in the hospital you are told to eat fifteen carbs when you are low and wait fifteen minutes. Then if you're still low, eat fifteen more and repeat until you are back in range.

So, this is what I did and it was a nightmare. I found myself experiencing the rollercoaster effect because as soon as I stopped going down, I was immediately going up. After bolusing to deal with the high, I would come crashing down and be back treating an urgent low.

I tried many different options before I came across glucose tablets. These tablets only have four carbs in them but each raises me by about 20 points and tends to stabilize me wherever I land. So, for instance, if I am at 65 mg/dL and trending steady, I eat one tablet and I usually level out at 85 mg/dL. This is perfect for me!

If I have a slow trend down but am still in range, I only need to eat enough to get me stable and keep me in range. However, if I am having an extreme low or trending low fast, I have to treat it differently. If I am extremely low or am in a place where I don't want to go very low, I will consume some fast-acting carbs and then eat one of my protein bars, because I know it easily impacts me by about 100 points. Now when I am trending down, all 100 of those points do not count toward a rise in blood sugar because some of the carbs are spent stopping the low.

For example, let's say I was at 100 mg/dL going down and ate a protein bar. The next two CGM readings put me in the low 70s. Then I start to rise and I level back off at 120 mg/dL. This shows that the protein bar kicked in to stop the low and then stabilized me. Those carbs counteracted the low so they shouldn't be considered something that needs an insulin bolus. And my Omnipod 5 pump will adjust the 120 mg/dL on its own back to my preferred blood sugar level; so I will wait to bolus and let it do its thing to ensure I am at a steady level before trying to make additional adjustments on my own.

Now that I am in college, some days I find that I am walking a lot between classes. If I am going low quickly, I grab an apple juice from the vending machines, drink some of it without covering any carbs and that levels me out without spiking me. This is because it is not only catching the low, but also providing me with quick energy as I walk around campus until I can eat a meal with protein. I also discovered the Transcend glucose gel packets and have two or three on hand at all times. These are great for when I am in the middle of an activity, such as taekwondo, and need a solution that will sustain me longer than the glucose tablets. The gel packets were created by a T1D and I love the idea of supporting someone who is also living with this disease.

Remember that different carbs raise your blood sugar differently. Ultimately, it's up to you to determine what foods you can eat and how they affect you.

I'LL TAKE A SIDE OF INSULIN WITH THAT

MICHELE

Let's face it, insulin is scary. Too much can kill you. Too little can kill you. And your body isn't always forthcoming with the answer. This whole disease is scary at first. But my attitude in general is the best way to overcome fear is to better understand the thing of which I am afraid. I wish it was as easy as "take a calculated dose of insulin at every meal and forget about it" like Jonathan's primary care doctor suggested it would be the day we learned of his onset. But it is not.

The type 1 diabetes (T1D) warrior training is very similar to a science experiment. Did I tell you I was a nerd? Oh, and I loved being in the science lab. I was the one in our group who willingly wrote up our scientific findings after every lab, so this training was right up my alley. Now the scientist in me deduced that the best way to decipher what Jonathan needed was to create a controlled environment. The main variable is the insulin usage. So the initial control was the food. This meant eating the same things every day until we got it right. I knew that once we deciphered this, we could move on to experimenting with other foods.

Another thing I thought about is food allergies. Consider this... if someone has a hard time processing peanuts or milk or gluten – we tell them to stay away from those foods. That makes sense, right? However, for people with T1D, whose bodies have a hard time processing sugar and simple carbs, we are told to eat whatever and bolus accordingly (insert mind-blowing emoji here).

Why would someone want to do that right after being diagnosed? Figuring out how to successfully manage T1D is so complex as it is, so why isn't the guidance to start easy and go for the harder stuff as you gain more confidence in what you are doing? I recognize that this may not be the long-term path for everyone, but why isn't it encouraged or recommended as an option for helping recently diagnosed individuals and caregivers get some quick wins under their belts early in the learning stage?

I know Jonathan will want to eat whatever at some point, but in the beginning, we took the path to first learn how to bolus with foods that are lower on the glycemic impact scale. Once we were able to solve those foods, we introduced ones with higher amounts of simple carbs and were better prepared to bolus correctly or correct the mistakes we made.

Start with the Basics

I am thankful that the keto and gluten-free diets are all the rage because their popularity gives people many more lower carb options than what used to be out there. I had been following a modified keto diet for the last four years, so I had a pretty good understanding of what it meant to eat low carb. However, I knew that Jonathan would want a greater variety of foods than what I ate – especially with his level of activity. So, we ordered different low carb foods and tried various keto recipes. We found out what brands and selections Jonathan preferred, and I placed auto-delivery orders and signed up for email/text discounts. Mostly I order directly from the product websites or Amazon; sometimes I can get items through our local grocery store.

Currently, our favorite low carb brands are *Quest, Zone Perfect, Siete, Magic Spoon, Livlo, Lily's, Sqwincher Zero, FairLife, Rao's, Ultima, Skinny Dipped, Catalina Crunch, Equip Protein, Healthy Noodles, Mr. Tortilla,* and *LC Foods*. If you live near an H-E-B grocery store, they have the best freshly made pro-keto tortillas that are the perfect flour tortilla substitute. There are so many other choices out there and many people swear by other brands for taste and glucose impact.

Some people love the brands I mentioned and others say these brands don't work for them. It really is a trial-and-error process and comes down to personal taste preference and individual glucose impact. Expect to pay more for some of these brands and items. I justify this for us because it gives Jonathan a better quality of life, reduces the amount of insulin he needs so his prescriptions last longer, and it keeps him healthier which translates into lower out-of-pocket medical costs for us. There are several Facebook pages managed by T1D caregivers and individuals who share low carb food options and bolusing techniques used to stay in a healthy glucose range.

I taught Jonathan to read the nutrition labels and how to measure everything so that he could eyeball foods when we were eating out or if he was at a friend's house. We purchased a food scale to ensure we had the correct portions. There are so many different food scales available and they are relatively inexpensive. There are even some that already have a couple hundred foods programmed so all you have to do is enter the food code and it will give you all the nutritional factors based on the weight of the item to minimize any miscalculations. Our practice has paid off to the point where we can measure a food by sight and then weigh it on the scale and only be off a gram or two.

So we measured and bolused, ate and tracked, and researched and learned for the first ninety days. I modified my personal recipes to account for almond flour and sugar alternatives, we tested many online recipes (in small batches) until we found our favorites and we noted the foods that tended to spike his glucose and removed them from his diet for the time being. A quick internet search for keto or low carb recipes results in several pages of really good sites. *All Day I Dream About Food* and *Wholesome Yum* are two sites I frequent on a regular basis. I like that their recipes are simple, use everyday ingredients and include the nutritional facts.

We watched videos, listened to podcasts, and overall absorbed as much as we could to learn how to have a healthy relationship with insulin and the T1D invader. One of my favorite sources I have found is the T1D informational podcast called *Juicebox Podcast* and the Facebook page called *Bold with Insulin*. These are both hosted by the same person. I recommend anyone who wants to become more of an expert at managing T1D to listen to his podcast and join his Facebook page. I've learned so much from these two sources including different ways to bolus, how to successfully eat the diet you want, conversations with others on their T1D journeys, and informative interviews with advice from diabetes experts. There is even an "after dark" series that focuses on adult topics such as sex, recreational drugs, mental illness, diabetic complications, addictions, self-harm and alcohol.

Pre- and Extended Boluses

Throughout all of my initial research, I uncovered that there are several different methods for bolusing and there are people who swear by all of them. You have to find out which one works best for your lifestyle and the way you eat. We also learned the importance of pre- and extended boluses which became a gamechanger for us.

If you think about it, it makes sense. Timing the digestion of the food with the absorption of insulin is required to avoid crazy highs and lows. Oh if I had a crystal ball for every insulin situation. I promise, I wouldn't use it for anything else, just to be more accurate in our boluses, timing, and know in advance of any oncoming highs and lows. Is that too much to ask?

It should be as easy as it sounds – but the math requires other variables. The type of insulin being used, the type of food being consumed, and how well the body is functioning that day all contribute to timing accuracy.

There are tons of charts online that provide insulin guidelines, expected onset of effect (how long before it starts working), when it peaks in the blood (maximum strength in terms of lowering glucose), and how long it lasts in the body. I noticed in all of the guidelines, regardless of the source, there are ranges for each data value – and some of those ranges are pretty vast. I pulled together the variances into one chart:

Insulin Type	Onset of Effect	Peak in Blood	Duration in Body
Rapid	5-15 min	30-120 min	3-5 hours
Short/Regular	10-30 min	2-8 hours	4-8 hours
Intermediate	2-4 hours	4-10 hours	10-18 hours
Long	1-4 hours	No peak	18-24 hours

This clearly illustrates that there is already an expectation that the absorption may be different depending on factors involved. I use this as a guide to find the most likely outcome for Jonathan and then set his baseline to experiment with other foods.

So for instance, when I packed Jonathan's lunch and snacks for school each day, I added a note with a carb count for each item. That way whether he chose to eat his whole meal or skip one of the items, he could bolus accordingly. Since he ate basically the same thing every day, it was pretty easy and he remembered his carb counts within a week. Each day we tracked each pre-bolus to determine what was the best timing to create the smallest inflection in his glucose line. For example, we learned that for best results, Jonathan needed to wait twenty to thirty minutes after he bolused to drink his morning protein shake since it was liquid and went through his system fast, even when he added almond milk. But he could eat his lunch in about fifteen minutes because the combination of food caused it all to digest slower and matched up better with when the insulin peaked. He was also more active after lunch, so that helped to minimize any glucose rise.

Counting Carbs

Figuring out carbs correctly is an essential part of insulin management success. If it is a processed food, the carb count is on the label. There are different thoughts on how to bolus for carbs – some people bolus for the entire carb count, some subtract the fiber portion and bolus for the remaining carbs. We bolus for all carbs minus any sugar alcohols because through trial and error we have discovered that those don't affect him. Using the example nutrition label, we would bolus nine carbs for each serving (fourteen total carbs minus five carbs for sugar alcohol).

Nutrition Facts	
Serving Size 1/2 Cup (64g)	
Servings Per Container 4	
Amount Per Serving	
Calories 70	Calories from Fat 20
	% Daily Values*
Total Fat 2g	3%
Saturated Fat 1g	5%
Trans Fat 0g	
Cholesterol 45mg	15%
Sodium 110mg	5%
Total Carbohydrate 14g	5%
Dietary Fiber 3g	12%
Sugars 6g	
Sugar Alcohol 5g	
Protein 5g	10%
Vitamin A 2%	Vitamin C 0%
Calcium 10%	Iron 2%
*Percent Daily Values are based on a 2,000 calorie diet.	

Sometimes I start with half a serving of a new food so I can test the impact of it. Sometimes I want fewer total carbs in the overall meal. And sometimes Jonathan's appetite calls for double the amount which is fine by me if the carb count is low or it is a complex carb. The key is to know how many servings he is consuming. Ensure you talk with your endocrinologist about which way you should calculate carbs. And if it isn't working for you, be willing to flex by either adjusting your insulin-to-carb ratios or how you determine carbs.

We use My Fitness Pal (only the certified entries) to determine the nutritional values regarding protein, fat and carbs with a goal of staying around thirty carbs per meal. My thought is that if we needed to increase insulin his glucose level wouldn't have gone too high to correct. And if we used too much insulin, it won't drop him too low as well. I've also been told that a good range to stay under is thirty to forty carbs because the body processes higher amounts of carbs differently once you get past that amount. That seems to be true for Jonathan. When we go over forty carbs, he tends to need to wait longer after he boluses to eat or he gives himself two separate boluses that equal the total number of carbs.

There are several nutrition trackers out there, so you need to find the one that works best for you. And if an entry looks off, then do an internet search, compare a few other sites, and go with what nutritional values are most often cited.

We always measure/weigh food prior to preparing it (straight out of the box or raw) and in accordance with the way it is factored (grams, ounces, milliliters, etc.) to ensure we calculate correctly. There are also online conversion scales to help convert between what is listed and what you want to use for measurement.

I know some of you are wondering why we track fat and protein in Jonathan's meals. This is because we use the total protein grams to calculate if there is a probability for a protein/fat rise later. Basically, if Jonathan is having a meal with something like a large steak and not much on the carbohydrate side, we take the amount of protein he is consuming in grams and then use a fourth of that for bolusing. For example, if he was eating eighty grams of protein and ten carbs, we might bolus as if he is consuming thirty grams of carbs. In MDI, we bolused for this after he finished eating since the protein takes longer to digest in his system. When we were on the Omnipod Dash insulin pump system, we would set up an extended bolus for these types of meals where we would bolus for the carbs upfront and then program an extended bolus to cover the protein over a couple of hours. The good thing about an extended bolus is that it can be canceled if it isn't needed and the pump stops giving that insulin bolus immediately. Now on the Omnipod 5 (O5), we bolus for the carbs up front and then bolus for the protein once he starts eating because extended boluses are only available in manual mode. While the O5 will eventually bring him into range, bolusing for the protein helps him get there much faster – and even stay in range on the days our calculations work perfectly.

As Jonathan has become more comfortable in knowing how his body reacts to food and food combinations, he has introduced more foods back into his diet mainly because he is working out to bulk and build muscle and he needs the additional calories. He has found that he doesn't enjoy many of the unhealthy and simple carb foods and chooses not to eat them. I realize that as he expands his diet, we will go through the process of chasing a high or catching a low while we evaluate the best way to bolus for these types of foods he chooses to keep in his diet – but we are no longer afraid of the process.

I know we are on the right path to a healthy relationship with insulin because over the summer he came home one day and asked me if I could guess what he ate while he was out with his friends. I looked at the Dexcom app and it had been a relatively steady, in range line all day.
"Okay, what did you eat?" I said curiously smiling.
"After the movies, my friends wanted food. So we went to a nearby restaurant and I ordered grilled salmon with asparagus and broccoli. Then we went to an ice cream shop and I got a scoop of 'no added sugar' vanilla and added strawberries. You didn't even notice." His grin was wide and he was very proud of himself.
"Oh my God. That is awesome. You never went above 140. How did you bolus for it?"
"I searched their websites, found the carb counts and then for the food, I bolused once the waiter said our order was coming out. For the ice cream, I bolused 60% while I was standing in line waiting to order with an extended bolus of 40% over one hour."

That was a good T1D day.

Food Tips

We learned that if we precook pasta or rice and then reheat it when preparing meals, the process makes the pasta/rice digest like a starch, thereby minimizing its normal glucose rise. We still bolus for the total amount of carbs, Jonathan just doesn't get the glucose rise. While Jonathan prefers his low carb pasta, this is good to know in case we are traveling or at a friend's house for dinner. I heard the same is true for white potatoes if you use a cooking process of boil/rinse/boil/rinse, but we haven't tried that as Jonathan has never cared for them.

Another tip is that not all fruit is created equal. We can't bolus for a Granny Smith apple the same way we bolus for a Gala apple. Same with a banana based on its ripeness. In this instance, it is not about the total carbs, but how fast they hit the body.

I remember in that first week or two after being diagnosed, I included some apple slices in Jonathan's lunch. He bolused "correctly" and then skyrocketed 100 points. Ugh. We walked away from all fruit except berries after that because obviously I needed to do some more research for that not to happen again. Now, he includes bananas in his protein shakes and enjoys peaches, melons, mangos, and grapes in moderation – because we have learned how to bolus for them.

Eating Out

We have found that when eating out, the best choice is to stay with simple meals – a grilled protein (usually fish, meat, or chicken) paired with grilled/steamed veggies and/or simple salad with dressing on the side. There are so many hidden carbs in restaurant foods that we often have to bolus up to twice as much as we would for the same meal if I make it at home. When we are out, we avoid sauces, complex entrees, most breads, and anything fried – even though he eats keto versions of these at home. We've tried it and it isn't worth the extra work to get his glucose back into range. If we know ahead of time that we will eat burgers, sandwiches or Mexican food, he might opt to take along his own hamburger bun or keto tortillas and replace the ones from the restaurant. On occasion, he takes a bite or two of a dessert that his brother orders just to get the taste or if he decides not to eat something on his plate and needs to cover the bolus. I love that he is disciplined enough to do that.

Many restaurant chains provide nutritional information on their websites which makes it easy for us to calculate his boluses. Other times, we guestimate or ask the chef or kitchen manager if they can estimate carbs for a certain portion of the plate. Most restaurants do what they can to help us. Worse case we bolus what we think and then give a correction bolus if Jonathan's glucose level starts to climb – as in straight arrow(s) up on his Dexcom based on what he has eaten. Also, depending on what he orders and when we expect the food to arrive, Jonathan pre-bolus either all or part of what he has calculated for carbs once the waiter has taken our order. Even if he has some insulin on board early, it helps if he has to wait to bolus for the rest when the food arrives.

Of course, some of the trickier foods are the ones everyone loves. These usually need extended boluses (pump) or an additional injection (MDI) due to the combination of protein, fat, and carbs in these tasty dishes. There are no set rules for these favorites either. Most of us start with this insulin bolus guidance and adjust as needed:

- Pizza/pasta: bolus for 30% of carbs immediately and remaining 70% over 2-3 hours
- Fast food: bolus for 70% of carbs immediately and remaining 30% over 1-1.5 hours
- Mexican/Chinese: bolus for 50% of carbs immediately and remaining 50% over 1-2 hours

For most of the first year, Jonathan avoided these typical restaurant foods, substituting some of his favorite dishes with lower carb options, testing with smaller portions, or choosing cleaner plate selections such as fajitas with grilled vegetables over enchiladas with rice and beans. He still hasn't tried Chinese and prefers the low carb alternatives we found for pizza. The only real fast food he eats is Chick-fil-a and he has his bolus for an 8-count nugget with a cool chicken wrap down to a tee. He's also become fond of a sugar-free vanilla latte with oat milk if hot and almond milk if cold.

Sometimes he may experiment with a new entrée if we are heading home afterwards and the weather is good. Because then if his glucose level begins to trend upwards, we can go for a long walk in our neighborhood to bring it back into range. In fact, the drive from the main exit to the front of our neighborhood is about half a mile and then we live another half mile from the front gate. In these instances, we get dropped off after turning from the main road and we walk back together. By the time we get home, he is most often in range and we can carry on with the rest of our day. I actually enjoy these walks so I don't mind when he wants to test a new meal. I get a chance to catch up with him, get some cardo, and digest my food as well.

Now don't get me wrong. I hate it when he is out of our preferred glucose range (70-140 mg/dL). But the truth is, I would rather him try new foods and go out of range while I am available to help him – then have him wait to try some of these foods when he is out on his own. Also, we are still relatively new to this, so there must be grace while he finds his way. I am sure with the strong foundational knowledge that we are building, as he moves into his adult life, he will continue to manage his glucose to maintain his A1C in the 5ish range that he has already achieved. And when we do have these moments, I remind myself that he is still in range 90+% of the time.

I'll pause here to state what is obvious but so often overlooked. I remind myself to do this at least once a week – it's really important to talk with Jonathan and hear what he has to say. As much as I am going through this with Jonathan, it is happening to him. I can empathize, but I am best at helping him when I understand what is happening to him straight from his mouth. Sure the numbers tell me a lot. But they do not tell the whole story.

One time when a new food had caused Jonathan to climb toward 200 mg/dL and we were walking our neighborhood to bring it down, he told me something that I hadn't read in any of the books or websites I researched.
"Mom, do you want to know how I feel when my sugar is out of whack?" he asked.

"Absolutely," I said.
"When it goes high really fast, it doesn't bother me, but coming down really fast makes me sick. On the other hand, going high really slow gives me a headache, but coming down really slow doesn't bother me. As far as going low, I can feel it once it hits in the 70s and is still going down, regardless of if it is dropping fast or slow, and that makes me nauseous. Coming back up is exhausting if I am down too long, even if it is steady – and that feeling can last hours even after I am in range."

"Thanks for sharing."

I gave him a hug as we rounded the corner and continued our walk. That was something I could have only learned by listening to him.

Water

I would be remiss if I left out how important water has been for Jonathan's insulin calculations. Water is an essential part of successful diabetes management – as it is for so many good things in life. Water is vital for helping the Dexcom accurately read glucose levels. If Jonathan is dehydrated, his readings are off. Period. Because the Dexcom measures the amount of glucose in the body's interstitial fluid and because that fluid accounts for about 40% of the water in the body, it makes sense that if Jonathan is dehydrated his glucose readings will be off. So better hydration, more accurate readings. If his Dexcom is off by more than 20 points, then we also push water when we calibrate. Adding sugar-free electrolytes to his water helps him consume more water and also get in essential minerals in the process.

Another reason water is so important for T1D management is that dehydration can produce a vicious cycle of elevated glucose levels. Water helps to dilute the glucose in the blood stream and process out the glucose through urine. If Jonathan is dehydrated, his glucose can rise higher than it normally would. Then the body starts grabbing water from anywhere it can to process out the glucose which leads to further dehydration, ketones, etc. We notice that when Jonathan is sick and his glucose level is elevated, he needs even more water than normal to help rehydrate him. Jonathan aims to drink about eighty ounces of water a day and then even more when he is active. He usually drinks a glass of water prior to every meal and then a glass before he goes to bed.

Finally, water helps to move insulin through the body. I think this is especially true for those who wear a pump because of the similarity to how it works compared with the CGM. I really don't know how to describe it. But often if Jonathan seems to be having a tough time with a spike and we have already bolused for the correct amount of insulin, he will drink a large glass of water before he boluses again to see if that helps – and most often it does.

Supplements

Along with adjusting Jonathan's diet, I also researched vitamins and minerals that he needs to add to his daily food intake. While he does eat a healthy diet, I recognized that we needed to examine what else the pancreas isn't doing (or struggling to do) for Jonathan, as well as understand how higher-than-normal glucose levels can impact the body on a daily basis.

I don't ever recall having lessons on the pancreas in biology class – it's one of those organs that no one really talks about until you need to talk about it. I stumbled upon the fact that in addition to producing insulin and glucose, the pancreas also produces enzymes that help the body digest food. Specifically Amylase for sugars and carbohydrates, Protease for proteins and Lipase for fats. I also discovered that high glucose levels can deteriorate gut health. Prebiotics and probiotics restore gut health, aid in digestion, and help decrease fasting glucose levels in those with T1D. Additionally, Jonathan's recent blood panel came back with a low level of Vitamin D even though he is outside quite a bit. So now he takes probiotics, digestive enzymes, Vitamin D/calcium, and a multivitamin daily to support his body and keep it functioning at an optimal level. We did share this strategy with our endocrinologist and she agrees with this extra nutritional support.

JONATHAN

I really enjoy food. And because of my workout schedule, I eat a lot. So figuring out how to bolus for the foods I want to eat is extremely important to me.

Early on, I did not enjoy my favorite foods because I didn't know how to bolus for them and they often made me skyrocket and stay high for hours. Because of this, I stuck to a very basic and nutritional diet focused on protein, complex carbs and fiber in order to get my bolusing correct.

I am glad my mom was willing to try so many different foods, recipes and brands to help me eat, in some resemblance, everything I enjoy and want to eat.

My mom made all sorts of new dishes for me to try. I appreciate that she willingly reworked the foods we ate so that they wouldn't spike me or leave me high for hours. Most of them were really great and we added them into our meal rotations. I didn't care for the low carb/sugar alternative dessert recipes because I still remember what they were supposed to taste like.

Because I ate so healthy for a very long time, when I was ready to try my favorite foods again, I found that I didn't like most of them anymore. Sugar was way too sweet after a few bites. Deep fried and greasy foods didn't sit well with me. And regular flour had a terrible aftertaste.

This makes my life easier because I am not tempted to eat unhealthy foods simply because I don't like them anymore.

We also signed up for a weekly fresh meal delivery that allows me to eat quality six-to seven-hundred calorie meals with a two-minute prep. Mom orders keto meals that have less than twenty carbs, so I can eat them anytime to keep my energy level high without worrying about my blood sugar doing the same. Often these are my go-to afternoon snacks or late-night meals after we eat dinner.

I have also found that if I go too long between meals, I tend to have the same feelings as if I am experiencing a low – even if my blood sugar is in a great range. My goal is to eat meals with no more than thirty to forty carbs in total, four to six times a day to help me have more balanced blood sugar levels. This way I am not giving myself large boluses.

Pre-bolusing can sometimes be a pain because I am either really hungry and want to eat right away or when we are out, I have to guess as to when I think my food will arrive. Honestly, I don't always wait like I should. I know that this decision might cause me to have elevated blood sugar, but I manage it by giving myself a little more insulin than what I would normally do to offset the timing imbalance. To compensate for not knowing how long the restaurant will take to bring my food, sometimes I bolus for one-third or half of the insulin I need and then wait to bolus for the rest when my food arrives. A lot of my decision has to do with how much insulin I think I need for the meal, what activity we will be doing afterwards, what my current blood sugar is at, and how long it takes to digest what I am eating.

My friends are really good about eating out at places that have better food choices for me. With the exception of Chick-fil-a, I really do not eat at fast food places because the grease is often too much for me. Plus it is extremely difficult to find healthy sides. When I do find myself having to eat at these types of places, I focus on the entrée and forgo the meal options – so just the protein and veggie toppings without the bun. Or I will order the gluten-free choices when available. This usually allows me to avoid high blood sugar spikes while hanging out with my friends.

Having an insulin pump does allow me to have more confidence in trying more complex foods because on the Omnipod Dash I could program extended boluses and on the Omnipod 5 I can program a temp basal. However, I found that I really didn't like most of the harder-to-bolus foods anymore. Pizza was a food I thought I missed. But surprisingly the doughy crust is too much for me and I choose not to eat it. I do eat flatbread pizza on occasion. We found a local brand where the crust is super thin. I add extra protein and vegetable toppings on it and then bake it for about ten minutes. Total carb count for the entire flatbread is around twenty carbs so that makes it easy to enjoy.

I've also learned to be better at drinking more water throughout the day. This seems to work best for my insulin movement. I notice that it takes the insulin longer to kick in and work when I am only drinking water with meals. Even though if you looked at ounces, it would be about the same – consuming the water equally throughout the day tends to produce better results. I don't count the water I drink during working out toward my daily consumption. So on workout days, I probably drink about 40% more water than on my "rest" days.

Michele Segura

I am glad my mom suggested adding vitamin supplements to my diet. I noticed a difference right away in how my body felt. I was less bloated and had more energy within a few days. I also notice that my body processes food better when I take them regularly. The best way for me to do that is to have them by my place at the dining table. I see them and it reminds me to take them without anyone saying anything.

BELOW THE CARB SURFACE

MICHELE

I found the notes portion of tracking Jonathan's daily insulin needs was about as important as knowing what food he ate. No one in the hospital or during our doctor appointments talked about all the other factors that impact a person's insulin sensitivity and needs. I don't know if they didn't want to scare us too soon with the complexity of this autoimmune disease or if it isn't widely well-known. I think the difficulty that comes with this disease being so personal makes it hard to teach doctors about all the factors beyond carbs.

In my research I have found that the most detailed recommendations come from others who are also type 1 diabetes (T1D) warriors. I ran across a chart at diatribe.org that shares 42 factors that affect blood glucose and it made so much more sense as to why the simple math I had been using didn't always create that beautiful glucose line we strive to achieve. It also further justifies the benefits of using an insulin pump to help us mitigate these other factors.

The chart shows how different factors such as food, medicine, activity, biology (sleep, illness, puberty, etc.), and the environment affect glucose. Most T1D conversations focus solely on food (mainly carbs) and an occasional mention of medicine interactions or cardio impact. These three categories don't cover half of the different factors. I also noticed that most every category increases vs decreases glucose levels. All the more reason we needed to best understand them to help mitigate constantly running at higher glucose levels than we want. I saw one parent post on a T1D Facebook page that her teenage daughter has four different weekly activity modes on her insulin pump that correspond to her menstrual cycle – and that's if everything else is "running normal".

Addressing the Other Factors

So I started documenting more data and making more adjustments. I watched for repeating trends on his Dexcom and created school, weekend, workout, sick and extremely active algorithm basal modes on his Omnipod Dash Personal Diabetes Manager (PDM). I continued to tweak them as we learned how to solve for his varying insulin needs throughout the day based on the situation. Even though we have moved to the Omnipod 5 and it runs on an automated mode, these are still programmed as manual modes for when he needs them.

We also used the different basal levels throughout the day to solve for what is referred to as the "dawn phenomenon" and "feet on the floor." While these two processes happen to everyone, those with T1D have to intentionally counteract the glucose rise because their body can no longer do it automatically.

Dawn phenomenon is the body naturally releasing hormones (e.g.: growth, cortisol, epinephrine, etc.) in the early morning. This tends to cause the glucose to rise. Using the CGM, we tracked Jonathan's glucose patterns for several days and then increased his automated insulin delivery around that time in the morning where we started to see the rise trend. Then we monitored that increase to ensure it leveled out his glucose line, making additional adjustments as necessary.

Feet on the floor is the liver's attempt to get energy to the body after sleeping and fasting. This happens as soon as the person starts moving around. Many adults with T1D have posted online that they choose to give themselves a bolus as soon as they get out of bed to take care of it. We chose to cover this by increasing his morning basal setting because he is a teenager and there is a strong chance he will forget that much needed bolus during his morning routines.

The **school mode** gives him a little more basal insulin between 7:30 am – 1 pm because he is sitting in class and less active. It then adjusts for slightly less insulin from 1 –10:30 pm to account for marching band practice and the continued insulin sensitivity he experiences afterwards. Finally, it is decreased further until midnight and then slightly increased to cover his natural glucose rises in the morning before he wakes.

The **weekend mode** is similar to the school mode but it gives Jonathan a steady dose of basal insulin throughout the day. He uses this mode when the weather recommends a pajama day watching movies or connecting with his friends through online gaming, because he needs more insulin to keep him in range when he is less active.

The **workout mode** has the amount of basal insulin drop off significantly in the afternoon and stay low throughout the night because he becomes very sensitive to insulin after he works out. I also adjust his insulin-to-carb ratios on these days to ensure he doesn't experience lows due to meal boluses. So instead of a 1:10 ratio, a 1:15 ratio seemed to work best for him. (I do this calculation manually as carb ratios can't be changed on the insulin pump for the different modes. In other words, if he wants to eat something with thirty carbs, we adjust the recommended bolus from three to two units before administering it.)

We initially thought he would use the workout mode for marching band, but that hypothesis was proven false. As the drumline captain, he not only had the performances to think about, but also corralling the other percussionists to be where they needed to be, when they needed to be there. Jonathan was born to play the drums and practices all the time. I love to hear him play and thankfully so does our neighbor. He took his leadership role seriously and was resolved to have the "cleanest line" during marching season. The adrenaline rush that came from his dedication actually made his glucose levels temporarily increase while marching around and carrying fifty pounds of drums. Even when he changed from tenor drums to snare drum (which is about ten pounds), the impact was the same. I thought the cardio would make him run low all the time, but we were more often pushing insulin during the cooler, evening football games and grabbing glucose tablets for the parades and marching competitions that took place in the heat of the day.

It did take a few games to determine the right amount of extra insulin he needed during his time in the stadium because once the game was over, his glucose level would tend to take a dive as the adrenaline was no longer pumping through his veins. We bolused in the first half of the football game if he was over 160 mg/dL and waited until we arrived back at the band hall before we decided if another correction was truly needed. Being the head chaperone for the marching band had its advantages once Jonathan was diagnosed with T1D. While I still had the responsibility of managing the successful travel for almost two-hundred teenagers, all the show props, equipment, instruments and uniforms to and from all games, performances and contests; it also meant I was able to be around when Jonathan needed me and could help him keep track of extra supplies so he could focus on his performances.

I remember his first marching contest after being diagnosed. I was down on the football field with the rest of the chaperones positioning our show props to take the field when the dreaded low alert beeped quietly in my pocket. I hadn't silenced my phone yet because we were still on the sidelines. I looked at my phone to discover that Jonathan was at 68 mg/dL trending down. At the same time, the band was now marching into the stadium to take their place on the sidelines in preparation for their performance. There was nothing I could do for the next twenty minutes. I tried to make eye contact with Jonathan, but he was already in performance mode. "I am sure he took care of it," I told myself. The announcer called our school and I gave my phone one last look. There was still one minute before the next reading. I turned my phone to vibrate and took the field to move my assigned prop into place. The band did great. We exited the field and I looked at my phone. 96 mg/dL. He had taken care of it.

We learned to carry low carb protein bars with us and he would eat one prior to warm-up without bolusing for the carbs and that would keep him pretty steady while he was marching in a contest or parade. He also planned for a fifteen- to twenty-carb snack after a football game to catch the dive if needed. He always kept glucose tablets in his uniform pocket, along with his Personal Diabetes Manager (PDM) device that he used to administer insulin through his pump.

We were introduced to the double whammy sick effect about nine months into his diagnosis when he tested positive for strep and the urgent clinic gave him a steroid shot along with some antibiotics. Not only did we have to increase his insulin because he was sick, but the steroid compounded his high glucose levels and we were at +30% temporary increase in basal insulin for about fourteen days. The first couple of days, I was quietly freaking out because no matter how many corrections we gave, his glucose level wasn't budging out of the 180-220 mg/dL range. I knew he felt awful from being sick and the high steady glucose range wasn't helping. So I turned to research and then called the endocrinologist's emergency phone number to confirm my plan with Jonathan's doctor. I set a temp increase by +10% and didn't see much movement even after getting up multiple times through the night to give additional corrections. The next day I went to +20% and started to see some improvement, but he was still staying in the 140-180 mg/dL range. On day three, we tried +30% and that seemed to be the magic number for that illness. He coasted down into the 90-130 mg/dL range and we both started sleeping through the night again. We kept the temp basal setting until he started experiencing a continual lower-than-normal trend in his glucose levels. It took almost a week after he completed his medication for that to happen.

This incident led me to create the *sick mode* on his Omnipod PDM where I pretty much increased his basal setting by about 0.1 u/hr. in every timeframe. It also sent me down another path of learning everything I could regarding what types of over-the-counter medications negatively affect T1D, which prescriptions are the best for T1D and how to best attack illnesses so that they don't impact Jonathan's glucose levels too much. One thing I have learned is to never assume any doctor is thinking about Jonathan's T1D during the initial thought of treatments. Even though his medical chart states he has T1D, we now remind the doctors about his T1D as soon as they begin discussing treatments and ask how the treatment will affect it. This technique alone has allowed us to avoid several mishaps of unfriendly prescriptions.

I've read a lot about surgeries and hospital stays as part of my research. And from what I can tell, if Jonathan ever has to encounter one of these situations, we will advocate to keep his pump and CGM on him because most hospitals/ surgery centers usually want to add insulin to the list of medications they manage for the patient. So far, no one I have come across has had a positive experience in these settings when they didn't continue to manage their own insulin needs. Most say the hospitals want to keep them around 200 mg/dL during the entire stay.

The last mode created for Jonathan is the **extremely active mode**. It provides the minimum amount of basal insulin the pod can administer and it is saved for times when Jonathan is hiking, biking, kayaking, or spending the day at an amusement park. We tested this mode with Jonathan before he set out on his own by going on a couple of local hikes with him. He wanted to find a mode that worked for him without suspending his insulin in case he ever forgets to turn it back on after the activity.

During his senior year, the band went to Orlando for Spring Break which included four days at amusement parks. It would be the first time Jonathan spent that amount of time in constant cardio since he was diagnosed as a T1D. We had no idea how he would respond.

There are tons of blogs on how to successfully manage Disney with T1D, including carb counts for favorite foods and special passes to help avoid standing in the long ride lines that drive glucose levels low. I probably read or skimmed through most of them while planning the trip. Some bloggers said they ran high all day because of the adrenaline. Some said they ran low because of the cardio. Several said they didn't change their basal settings at all. Okay... so again... this was going to be personal and something we would need to determine once we got there.

We did apply online for the assistance passes (Disney DAS pass and Universal AAP pass) ahead of our trip. I highly recommend doing this online vs waiting until you get to the parks. You will be given an approval code or reference number that you give the onsite Guest Relations clerk and they then hand you the pass without question. It saves a lot of time and frustration. The best way to get approved is to say something along the lines of "the request is due to a chronic health condition that can require the need to frequently exit the lines to use the restroom and safely treat blood sugar levels that can cause dizziness, vomiting and sickness." Just saying "type 1 diabetes" doesn't work because the person on the other side of the phone or chat doesn't understand all that diabetes management entails and often confuses it with type 2 diabetes which is usually denied.

Up until the trip, Jonathan had remained private about having T1D. But he did decide to tell the friend group he was rooming and hanging out with at the parks in the event he needed help. They were surprised and asked questions because they had spent so much time with him and never realized that anything had changed over the last two years. They were also supportive. That gave Jonathan great comfort to know his friends didn't judge him or treat him differently.

During the bus ride, he set a temp basal of +20% because he wasn't active and therefore it would be harder for his body to burn off the extra glucose. He also knew he wasn't going to get much sleep and would need the extra insulin. He probably could have increased the temp basal even more, but we agreed before the trip that he would manage everything on his own and would let me know if he needed help. So I didn't say anything. He hung out in the mid to upper 100s for most of the ride there. This was the toughest part of the trip because we were on the buses for almost twenty-four hours straight during the drive down to Orlando and then again for the drive home. We would stop to eat but were usually back on the bus within the hour. So Jonathan had little opportunity to exercise after eating. After a couple of pesky highs, he asked me if he should bolus on the heavier side when he ate and I agreed.

Once we arrived in Orlando it was the complete opposite. He stayed in our preferred range almost the entire time while running around the parks with his friends. He tested how to best adjust his insulin management during that first day and only had to treat a couple of lows while he was there. His solution? Jonathan kept his PDM on the extremely active mode and rarely bolused for anything he ate under twenty carbs. For larger meals, he gave himself partial boluses. Most of his snacks came from his personal supply and he used our "eating out" meal strategy since he already knew how those types of food affected him.

He calculated all of this on his own. While I was on the trip and often in the same park as him, I rarely saw him. I was busy helping to solve student and chaperone concerns that arose throughout each day. I mainly saw him at night during room checks or when he came by to change out his Omnipod as he kept his T1D supplies in my room.

JONATHAN

T1D isn't the worst disease, but it's also not the easiest to handle. While I did enjoy the pleasant doctor visits in the hospital, I soon found out that there was much more to managing diabetes than what I was told.

The doctors focused their conversations solely on food and mainly carbs. I think this leads many people to misunderstand T1D as a "food/metabolism disease". Foods do play a big role in successfully managing T1D. This is true. But what doctors forget to tell you or don't know themselves is that carbs aren't the only thing you have to count. You can also have a blood sugar rise from protein and fats in the foods that you eat. And then, of course, there is everything else.

I came to realize that T1D is affected by so much more than food. You have to consider if you slept well enough the night before, have had enough food and water throughout the day, have been active, and have had enough insulin. My life revolves around diabetes every second of the day. Things did get better once I got my CGM and insulin pump and my mom determined how to adjust my basal settings to keep me in a better range. But it is still something I have to think about more than I like.

As quickly as I learn everything and even when I am doing everything correctly, my blood sugar can still get out of line for no apparent reason. Or I can simply not feel well from the effects of medicine, growing, allergies, stress, etc. Not every ache and pain I feel is diabetes related, but everything can affect my T1D.

Creating the different basal modes was extremely helpful and also taught me to better understand how what I did affected my insulin needs. Now that I am on the Omnipod 5, I have those modes programmed in the manual setting if I need them. About once every six months I sit down with my mom and we review my bolus history and then make adjustments to the formulas to coincide with my current basal/bolus needs. The mode we make the most adjustments to is the sick mode. We always calculate about a 30% increase to my current basal average to help me stay in range when I am not feeling well.

Being sick with a stomach bug for the first time taught me more about T1D. That was an awful experience because I kept throwing up no matter what I tried. Of course not feeling well along with not being able to hold down any food caused my glucose to skyrocket. My mom kept pushing clear fluids and electrolytes, as well as having me check my pee for ketones. Luckily, I didn't have any. When we were finally able to get my blood sugar level down, I was terrified because it kept going down. Either my pancreas had kicked in and was trying to help or my body needed energy that I couldn't give it.

I remember thinking to myself, "I'm going to have to go to the hospital with an extreme low". Finally, I was able to drink a small protein shake despite experiencing a gagging sensation with every sip. I managed to keep it down long enough for my blood sugars to level out. After that, I started to get better and the immediate scare was over.

IT ISN'T STACKING IF YOUR BODY NEEDS IT

MICHELE

Stacking was one of the terms I heard in the hospital. Don't do it. Avoid it at all costs. Wait until the insulin is out of him before giving him more. Stacking is when you give the body too much rapid-acting insulin because you are making corrections on top of corrections which could result in hypoglycemia. The basic guidance is to wait three hours after giving insulin to give a correction bolus. This is where the sliding scale comes into play (1 unit of insulin for every 30 above 130 mg/dL or 40 about 140 mg/dL or 50 above 150 mg/dL, etc.). I completely understand this and agree with the thought process. To me it makes sense if all the stars are aligned with how we bolused. I understand the body has to do its thing and that takes some time.

But what if I messed up and didn't bolus correctly? What if my crystal ball was cloudy that day? I mean I am just deciphering all this out and clearly I am making mistakes if he is out of a healthy glucose range for a long period of time. Why should his glucose range stay high because we didn't get the bolus amount right? Why does he have to feel awful for at least two to three hours? And what if he wants to eat again before three hours? Does he have to wait? It didn't make sense, but I wasn't knowledgeable at the time to ask the right questions about it.

While reading posts in various online groups, someone shared the incorrect bolusing results provided by an endocrinologist. And I saw it again and again, slightly different, but also the same. So I knew it was worth exploring. We use this basic guidance to adjust for how we are bolusing and to determine how to give corrections to keep Jonathan in a healthy glucose range:

- **Early boluses** (too much time between pre-bolus and eating) most likely create low levels within an hour after eating, followed by a rapid spike. We learned to compensate for this by an additional bolus or a good long walk once the arrow on his Dexcom turns upward.

- **Late boluses** (not enough time between pre-bolus and eating) generate a rapid glucose spike soon after eating but mostly likely comes down on its own. In this situation, we decided that we should wait about two hours to see where Jonathan is trending and then adjust accordingly.

- **Weak boluses** (perhaps calculation was too low or we didn't properly adjust for the type of carb/meal) result in high but steady glucose level after eating. After trial and error we learned that once I see that Jonathan's glucose level is steady but high, we resolve it with an additional bolus or exercise.

- **Large boluses** (miscalculation of carb intake or overcompensating for type of carb/meal) create low glucose levels two to three hours after eating. We usually see this on his Dexcom as either a downturned arrow or a steady decrease in glucose level. When this happens, we treat with additional food or glucose tablets depending on where we think he will land.

As for eating too soon, we realized that just because he has type 1 diabetes (T1D) he isn't limited to eating only three or four times a day. He can eat as often as he wants and we should always bolus for what he eats unless we are catching a low. So if he wants a snack thirty minutes after eating lunch, we ignore the Dexcom reading and bolus only for the amount of carbs in the snack. This allowed us to cover his carbs without stacking insulin based on the current glucose level which was already calculated in the first bolus.

Daytime Corrections

Giving correction boluses during the day doesn't make me nervous. It did at first, but we have done enough analysis on what does and doesn't work for Jonathan, that I feel pretty confident to take the right steps should he go low. We have the supplies we need and we know how to adjust and get him back into range.

I only worry about giving him corrections during the day when he is in an environment where he doesn't have the ability to control the situation. For example, taking an exam, at a seated event or when he is performing. During those times, Jonathan usually gives himself about half the amount of correction he would normally give so he doesn't have to worry about a glucose crash in a setting where he can't easily take control of the situation.

Another solution we have found is that if Jonathan is sitting with a higher than desired glucose level and he can't get up, doing soleus push ups – basically sitting calf raises with a two-count squeeze when his legs are at the highest level of the lift – helps to lower his glucose. We have watched his glucose level drop by four points at a time by doing these for a few minutes without bolusing any extra insulin. It's a pretty neat trick and most people won't even realize you are doing it.

Nighttime Corrections

On the other hand, it took me a long time to get comfortable with giving correction boluses at night. I mean I want to sleep. Jonathan wants to sleep. The alerts had already woken me up. Now I had to stay up and make sure I didn't overdo the correction. We found the best thing to do to avoid having to deal with correction boluses during the night is to stop eating at least two hours before bedtime. The goal is to have the food digested and no extra insulin on board. If this is true, then we have glorious straight-line, blissful deep sleeping nights.

Of course this only works if you have determined your correct basal settings. So if you are still running high or dipping low overnight, then you need to work with your endocrinologist to adjust your basal settings. Outside of the first month or so after being diagnosed (while basal settings are still being adjusted), I don't think anyone should have to consistently rely on additional food at bedtime just to keep steady and not experience dangerously low glucose levels.

This pattern of eating two hours before going to bed worked well in high school because Jonathan had a pretty set schedule most days. However, once he entered college that schedule went out the window along with when he ate. His first class each day started mid-morning so I never knew if he was going to get up in time to have breakfast or rush out the door with a protein shake in hand. We still try to eat dinner as a family, but that means sometimes dinner is closer to 8 pm once everyone gets home from evening classes. And then there is late night studying, playing computer games until the wee hours of the morning, or hanging out with friends – in other words, normal college student life. All of these often come with a rumbling stomach of a growing boy who easily will consume another five hundred calories after dinner and then fall into bed without another thought.

In these instances, I encourage foods that we know have minimal impact on him. But often I am already in bed when he makes his way into the kitchen for something to eat. He may have a perfect glucose line when I shut my eyes, only for me to be awakened by his high notification alert and the effects of a late-night meal eaten too soon after bolusing.

Moving to the insulin pump made a huge difference in giving night corrections. First of all, I didn't have to wake up Jonathan. If he is running higher than we want, I use the Personal Diabetes Manager (PDM) to give him a correction while he sleeps. Secondly, his PDM helps my sleepy head calculate the recommended bolus. Again, the importance of knowing your numbers so you can correctly program them into the pump technology. And third, when we transitioned to the Omnipod 5, the algorithm stops giving him insulin if it expects his glucose level is going low which gives me additional comfort.

These corrections help him sleep better. He told me staying high all night was kin to only getting a few hours of sleep. Experiencing a night of high glucose levels means waking up exhausted, with a headache and definitely not prepared to be his best that day. If no one has told you, sleep is more important for those with T1D than most people realize. Not getting enough sleep can greatly increase one's insulin sensitivity making it harder to stay in range during the next day. We have found that when Jonathan has a restless night or gets less than six hours of sleep, he needs about 20-30% more insulin during the next twenty-four hours than what he normally uses. That's huge! So we strive for going to bed without extra insulin on board and correct as needed so that he can have his best day, every day.

JONATHAN

When I was in MDI, I really didn't like to give myself correction boluses. I don't like shots, so I usually waited until I was about to eat something and do it all at once. That way I was only giving myself shots four or five times a day. Having the Omnipod pump has made it so much easier to give myself corrections when I need them. The nice thing about the pump is that it gives me a suggested correction amount. Early on, that helped me build confidence in treating highs.

My mom taught me to be aggressive with corrections. I used to wait until my blood sugar leveled off wherever it landed and then correct it. Sometimes that meant waiting a couple of hours before I took any action. However, now I start correcting when I see it trending upward and then about an hour after I have eaten if it isn't coming down. Not only does this help me stay in range longer, but since I now have the Omnipod 5, it helps the algorithm learn that I don't want to stay in the higher ranges for too long. Being in tune with my body has also helped me know if the pump bolus recommendation is too aggressive or not aggressive enough based on the many other factors that I take into account that the pump can't consider. This enables me to successfully make adjustments to the pump recommendations and land at a desired level.

I don't always treat high blood sugar levels with insulin if there are other ways available to bring it down. This may be achieved by playing drums, being active, or heading to the gym. My mom also purchased a treadmill that I use during

Michele Segura

bad weather days or when it is late at night. Sometimes I give a partial correction and then use an activity to bring me the rest of the way into my preferred range.

Regarding nighttime corrections, the Omnipod 5 does a really good job of keeping me in a tight range while I sleep. This has helped me get far better rest than what I was getting early in my diagnosis. I used to tell my mom not to worry about correcting my level if I was under 150 mg/dL. Even though my blood sugar was higher than I liked, I would still get a good night's sleep in this range. And usually, through my basal settings and my partially active pancreas, I would get to my desired range by the time I woke up. If I am above 150 mg/dL I need a correction or I wake up groggy with a headache. When I don't wake up to my Dexcom alerts, my mom is really good about bolusing an insulin correction for me to get me back into my desired range. Even though she is quiet when she comes into my room, I sometimes wake up depending on where I am in my sleep cycle. However, since it is so easy to give a correction bolus with the Omnipod, I fall right back to sleep and sometimes by the morning I forget that it happened.

STAYING ACTIVE

MICHELE

Jonathan is an active teenager. So when he was diagnosed, I knew I needed to decipher how he could continue to be active and manage his glucose levels effectively. At the time, he was the drum captain for his high school marching band and played drums in the jazz band. He was also into recreational sports (hiking, basketball, kayaking, and paintball) and had joined a local gym. I wanted him to be able to continue doing all of these things and more. He wanted to be able to do these things and not think about his type 1 diabetes (T1D).

About four weeks into Jonathan's diagnosis, I was lucky enough to stumble upon the website, Diabetic Athletic. Coach Nick and I exchanged emails and a few zoom calls before he talked with Jonathan. As a thirty-year T1D veteran and former body-building competitor, he had the personal experience to train Jonathan to be his best self. Nick understands first-hand the challenges that come with being active with T1D.

We signed up for his online training program and I was really pleased to watch the physical, emotional, and mental transformation Jonathan underwent over the next few months. Jonathan has become more knowledgeable about how to plan for being active as well as what to expect while being active. We have also recognized that Jonathan's insulin sensitivity can be extremely high resulting in minimal insulin needs up to twenty-four hours later.

In talking with Jonathan, he told me the one thing he wishes newly diagnosed young adults knew is that they don't need to be afraid to workout and be active. He was at first, but now knows that he can do anything he wants if he prepares himself for it. He is successful because he is first willing to go slow and test how he reacts to new activities.

When he is trying new activities and isn't sure how his glucose will be affected, he intentionally stays a little higher in range than normal. He says that being around 150 mg/dL in those situations helps him keep his edge in case he needs to abandon the situation. A good example is the first time he tried jet skiing. We were out in the ocean and he wanted to ensure that if he needed to swim, he would have the stamina to do it. So he ate a protein bar without bolusing for it and enjoyed the next four hours jet skiing with his friends. He also wore his Dexcom and Omnipod the entire time. While he did stay in the mid to upper 100s while jet skiing, he coasted back into our preferred glucose range once he returned to the beach house, showered and cooled down. Was it perfect? No. Did he make great memories? Yes. We are still learning. For us, we consider this data collection to use for the next time.

Regarding working out. When Jonathan has a tough weightlifting set ahead of him and he hasn't eaten in a few hours, he consumes about thirty to forty carbs one hour before working out. If he has recently eaten, he only consumes about ten to fifteen carbs. One thing that has changed for him is that he used to enjoy working out in the mornings. However, he can no longer do that because his body doesn't hold on to carbs like it did before his onset of T1D. Now he needs food on board to give him the strength and stamina to have an effective workout. Additionally, for heavy sets, his coach recommends that he has more insulin on board (IOB) because the heavy lifting actually increases his glucose levels. Overall, he aims to be between 140-160 mg/dL before beginning his workouts.

However, if he is participating in a more aerobic or cardio workout, he tries not to have any extra insulin on board. This is true when he goes hiking, kayaking, bike riding or plays basketball. Usually he plans to consume five to twenty carbs every so often during these activities. He also eats a meal with about thirty to forty carbs and a good portion of protein with a small bolus before beginning these activities. The protein helps to stabilize his glucose level and the carbs give him quick energy to burn. Often, he puts his pump on the "extremely active" mode if we know it will be a long day.

Regarding other activities he participates in regularly:

- **Paintball** often gives him an adrenaline rise so he has to watch for elevated glucose levels. Additionally, the full body padding and helmet in the Texas heat can dehydrate him faster. The combination of the two is something he watches pretty closely during the first thirty minutes or so, sometimes bolusing to add

IOB to counter the rise. After that, the effect of the extended cardio kicks in and his glucose level begins to drop. To solve for this, he trades off between drinking water and low carb electrolytes. He also is careful to cover his CGM and insulin pump to avoid them being damaged during play. He does this by ensuring they are both on the front of his abdomen and then covers them with a padded belt that also holds his extra paintballs.

- **Fishing and golf** have no impact on his glucose (we walk for nine holes and use a cart for eighteen holes). What is important is that he knows how long he plans to be out because his main focus is staying hydrated. He also eats a small snack without bolusing every couple of hours to maintain his energy.

- **Kayaking** only affects him if he stays out in the water past an hour. By then, his constant padding will usually kick in the cardio effect on his glucose level. He treats pending lows with glucose tablets. He also uses a watertight bag to hold his PDM, glucose tablets and protein snacks. This protects them from getting wet and the bag floats if it falls in the water.

- **Taekwondo** has a mixed effect. When he is sparring, we have to balance his adrenaline rise with the intense one minute rounds of fighting. He needs enough energy to successfully spar, but increased glucose levels can make it hard for him to concentrate. Our strategy is to have a healthy meal an hour or so before he spars and then balance his glucose levels between the rounds with glucose gels or tablets. Like paintball, he also ensures the placement of his devices are protected by the padding. When he is teaching or practicing his forms, he does not adjust his insulin.

- **Basketball, hiking and bike riding** keep him low. He eats a protein snack before starting and drinks electrolytes throughout the activity. His goal is to have no additional IOB from a previous meal. He keeps additional snacks available for breaks and afterwards to keep him stable.

- **Swimming and snorkeling** will impact him after about twenty minutes in the water. He will begin to trend low about this point in time and the pace will increase afterwards. If he is swimming, he treats his pending glucose lows similarly to how he manages kayaking. If he is snorkeling, he will eat protein and fast-acting carbs before he gets into the water and then monitor his level about every thirty minutes.

- **Hot tubs and steam rooms** tend to drop him while he is in them. If they are hot enough to make him sweat, he starts with a small glucose rise due to the intense heat on the body. After that, he trends low as he sweats. The key for him is to not stay in too long. If he stays in for the recommended fifteen to twenty minutes, then once he gets out, his levels balance out on their own. If he stays in longer, he will need to treat for a low glucose level.

Recently after a bout of the flu, Jonathan resumed his training routine. He knew what he needed to do. He felt he had the experience to get it right. But his glucose levels were all over the place. His body still had residual effects from the recent illness and over-the-counter medications. Because of this, after completing his first set he had to stop and eat since his glucose level was trending low faster than usual. This concerned him and he halted training before finishing the scheduled workout. When he came home, we talked about what had happened at the gym. He realized that he had lost track of the basics and spent the rest of the week approaching the workouts as if he was doing them for the first time. This enabled him to get back on track and by the following week he was able to resume his normal training program without any issues. He said he wants active teens with T1D to know not to give up. Understand what's not working. Go back to the basics until you get it right.

JONATHAN

While all of this knowledge helped me in understanding how to be active it also made me more aware about how much my life had changed. I realize now that even when I go shopping with my friends or family, I have to watch my blood sugar because the extensive walking can cause my sugar to crash. I even realized that something as simple as getting on stage for a concert can cause my sugar to rise because I am stressed or nervous.

One time a friend of mine told me how lucky I was because "I get to eat sweets all the time". I reminded him that "I don't get to" eat sweets, "I have to" eat glucose whenever I am experiencing a low because my body can no longer produce it on its own. It bothers me that some people think like that because I never really ate many sweets before being diagnosed. And honestly eating sweets all the time would wreak havoc on my T1D.

I remember trying to get back into the gym after being diagnosed. I woke up, had a protein bar (bolused for it obviously), and then had a terrible workout. I was lightheaded and felt like I wanted to cry for no reason. Another day I was feeling really good and I wanted to lift heavy. But after a few heavy sets, I started to get a headache, felt sleepy, and overall didn't feel well. "What the heck was going on?" I thought. These feelings absolutely scared me but I wanted to get stronger. I tried a couple more times each resulting in a different outcome. I didn't know what was going on at the time, but now I know that it was due to my blood sugar going too low and too high as a direct result of the type of workout I was doing.

My mom did a lot of research to find a knowledgeable T1D trainer who had my best interests in mind. With his help I was able to get back into my weightlifting routine and build muscle while staying in a healthy blood sugar range. He also guided me in how to take care of my blood sugar while being active and how different levels of activity can change everything about your diabetes.

Let me explain.

When you are active your body is forced to use its glucose reserve. This is because glucose is a fast energy solution for the body. An active body also increases blood flow to the muscles in the digestive system, which massages our food along the digestive tract – a process known as peristalsis –causing it to work more quickly and effectively.

Also during exercise, your body burns glycogen, a form of glucose that is stored in your muscles. After exercise, your muscles replenish its glycogen storage with glucose from the bloodstream. The more glycogen that is burned during an activity, the longer the body's insulin sensitivity is improved. This means you have to use less insulin when bolusing for meals and less insulin in general for up to twenty-four hours after exercising.

Of course, if you take days off, then that insulin sensitivity goes away. This is why I believe fitness is a type of natural medicine that makes staying active important to those with T1D. For me this means going to the gym.

Many people don't realize the benefits of being active. They think it's about getting strong, bulky, slimming down, or becoming faster. But it also improves your brain health, decreases your risk of chronic conditions (like type 2 diabetes, heart disease, and many types of cancer), reduces depression, anxiety, and dementia, and strengthens bones and muscles. For those of us with T1D, it's a great source of lowering blood sugar and making our bodies adapt to being active so we don't experience as many low crashes and high rises.

When I am doing cardio activities, I burn more sugar. This includes activities such as bike riding, walking/running, and working out with sets that consist of twelve reps and higher. To help ensure I am prepared in these situations, I wear a crossbody bag that contains snacks, glucose tablets and gel packets, and my Baqsimi.

On the other hand, some workouts, such as heavy weightlifting, sprints, and competitive sports like taekwondo sparring, cause me to produce stress hormones (such as adrenaline). Adrenaline raises blood sugar levels by stimulating your liver to release glucose. I have to be careful when determining the need for insulin as all of these activities require energy, so after the rise I tend to come down resulting in a sugar crash if I don't manage my insulin.

One time well into my training program, I started feeling weird. I had no energy and was struggling to focus during classes. It was odd because my sugars were absolutely perfect. No one seemed to know what was going on. Even my doctors were unable to help me. When I shared this with my trainer, he told me that it was because I wasn't getting enough food compared to the number of activities and the intensity of the activities that I was doing every day. So I started eating more often and increased my total calorie intake. After that simple fix, I was back to my normal self.

THE DEMONS OF HIGHS AND LOWS

MICHELE

I've heard that the best way to be in control of your life is to live it with discipline and moderation. This is especially true for type 1 diabetes (T1D) management. While some may argue there are normal fluctuations in glucose levels for everyone, I would suggest that those variations are hills compared to the steep mountains and valleys that are commonplace in the T1D world. My research indicated that the normal glucose variance for teenagers and young adults is around 30-40 mg/dL vs swings in the hundreds. As we have discussed throughout the book, staying in a good range helps maintain good energy levels, better moods, and an improved quality of life. So we aim for Jonathan to maintain a variance of less than 40 mg/dL on a daily basis.

I mentioned earlier how Jonathan can sense when his glucose is trending out of range – either high or low. This is possible because we do what we can to keep him in range and steady. While conducting my research, I discovered that people who let themselves have severe and frequent out-of-range glucose levels actually have less ability to know when they are experiencing an extreme high or low. In this situation, the brain starts operating as if the rollercoaster ranges are normal and no longer signals that something isn't right.

When I read about the impact of rollercoaster glucose levels on the brain's ability to signal the body that something is wrong, I realized this is one more reason to keep Jonathan in a healthy range as much as possible. Aside from all the immediate benefits of feeling good and the long-term benefits of having a healthier life, accepting the rollercoaster as normal puts him at risk of having a severe hypoglycemic episode and not catching it in time because his body won't alert him that something is wrong. Yes, the Dexcom would send alerts but that doesn't mean he will react to them appropriately if he thinks he feels fine because his brain is no longer signaling any concerns.

Because we focus on keeping him within normal glucose ranges, Jonathan can actually feel changes in his glucose levels before it shows up on his Dexcom continuous glucose monitor (CGM) or before the Dexcom or Omnipod 5 insulin pump predicts it. Sometimes this can be up to thirty minutes before the trend starts. This is extremely helpful because it allows him to better prepare for what is coming. Sometimes we go for a walk if he feels his glucose level is about to go high or he watches for the Dexcom arrow to turn slightly down and then treats the pending low glucose level.

Tightening the Range

If you don't have tight ranges set for the CGM alerts, your glucose can get out of hand quickly. Our goal is to keep Jonathan in the tight glucose range we have determined as our preferred range so that when things go haywire, the craziness isn't so bad. It is much easier to get control of a high glucose level with a 150 mg/dL alert than a 200 mg/dL alert, so we have his alert range set tighter on his CGM than what his endocrinologist recommends. Technically, he is in a good medical range from 70-180 mg/dL, but on my Follow app, I have him set at 70-140 mg/dL so my alerts go off once he is out of this range for more than fifteen minutes.

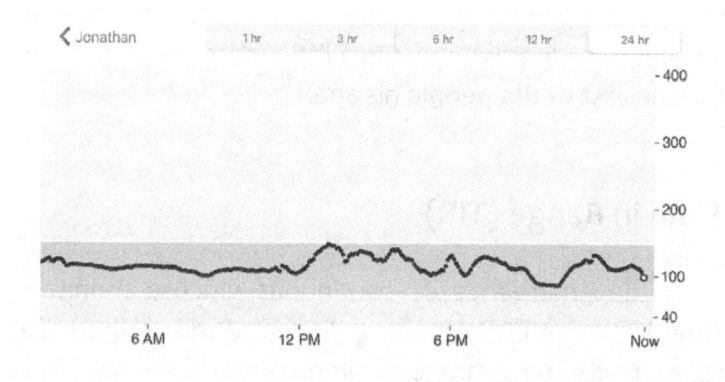

Jonathan has his alert range set from 85-160 mg/dL. He has his lower level set higher so he can get ahead of potential lows. This is especially helpful when he is active because the glucose dive can happen quicker than normal. He has his top number set a bit higher than mine to minimize an alert sounding while he is in class or working out. He says he still feels when he starts to go high and will give himself a bolus correction once he gets above 150 mg/dL, but at least the alerts won't be going off in his pocket and disturbing others.

The nice thing about the Omnipod 5 is that it automatically reads the Dexcom level. So if he is trending high, he hits the "CGM reading" button and then lets the system bolus according to how much insulin is already on board and how it expects him to trend over the next hour. And if he is trending low or expected to go lower than our preferred range, it suspends insulin to help keep him from dropping too low.

I would love to see him target a tighter range with a high alert of 120 mg/dL or even 110 mg/dL. But I recognize the level of discipline that this would entail and he is, after all, a college student who wants a little more freedom to be like the rest of the people his age.

Time in Range (TIR)

With the emergence of continuous glucose monitors, Time in Range (TIR) is being discussed more often. TIR refers to the percentage of time your glucose level is in your targeted range and should be considered along with your A1C. The difference between the two is that while the A1C measures the average blood glucose over a two to three month period; it cannot capture the amount of time spent in various glucose ranges throughout the day. This means that a person could have a low A1C number, but what looks like diabetes management success is masked because the extreme lows negate the extreme highs.

However with a CGM, people can track the time they stay in a healthy glucose range. The American Diabetes Association recommends that people with diabetes should try to stay in a healthy glucose range (80-180 mg/dL) for 70% of the day. Our endocrinologist has told us that when Jonathan moves out of the honeymooning phase, we may have to work harder to keep him in the 90+% range he is currently experiencing. I believe that with the knowledge we are gaining, we will be able to solve this when that time comes.

Short-term Impacts

It's not only about long-term consequences that the medical community focuses on when discussing high glucose levels. We hear so much about complications such as retinopathy, cataracts, glaucoma, kidney disease, neuropathy issues, strokes, cognitive impairments, coronary heart disease and lack of blood flow in his arms and legs due to extended high glucose levels. We are told it takes a while for those to develop so not to worry about them too much for now. And honestly, because we focus on staying in a healthy glucose range, we don't.

What we do worry about is how Jonathan feels and his ability to think and function normally throughout each day. The healthy glucose range (80-180 mg/dL) suggested for those with diabetes doesn't work for Jonathan.

When Jonathan's glucose is running close to 180 mg/dL or higher, it gives him a headache. He feels tired and sluggish. His heart races. He is irritable and quick to anger.

He is anxious. It is hard for him to sit still and focus. These times are tough. The diabetic rage is real. I know the things he says and does during these times aren't him. He apologizes for his rudeness or anger once he feels better – but that makes him feel worse in a different way. Additionally, because he feels like he does, it is harder to do the activities most recommended to lower his glucose such as jumping on a trampoline, jumping jacks, squats, etc. What works best for him is something low intensity – walking, treadmill, stationary bike or playing the drums. Yes, even with a headache, he sometimes opts to play the drums. Twenty minutes on the drum set can drop him 30-40 points.

When Jonathan's glucose is running below 80 mg/dL, he becomes intensely emotional. He can get sad. He is shaky. He feels hungry even if he just ate a full meal. And his body wants to relieve itself of everything already digested. If he has been sleeping, he can be obstinate and disoriented when we wake him.

These are generally the feelings that accompany Jonathan's highs and lows, but he tells me that these symptoms change occasionally either because his body has adapted or changed over time.

Watching this happen to Jonathan early on reminded me of when I was in my twenties and had debilitating migraines. This is another health condition whose effects go unseen by those around you. At the time there wasn't much knowledge on how to treat migraines. I saw numerous doctors and endured countless treatments that never resolved the issue. My migraines controlled me. I had them almost daily. They lasted for hours making it hard for me to focus. Then they would leave me drained and exhausted after finally subsiding. They could be brought on by excessive activity, a reaction to a food I ate, or wake me unexpectedly in the middle of a quiet slumber like a nightmarish prank. While I learned to successfully function even during the worst of those days, the migraines did absorb most of my joy. I was always trying to ensure the last uninvited migraine was gone for good or looking over my shoulder for the next one to show up. There were many things I wanted to do but couldn't because of how miserable I felt. I traded too many social invitations for a dark, quiet place that could dull the sharp migraine cutting through my head.

I don't want that for Jonathan. I don't want him to be exhausted by out-of-range glucose levels. I don't want T1D to prevent him from hanging out with his friends and enjoying his favorite activities. I don't want T1D to steal his joy. I want him to experience life and create lasting memories. This is where discipline and moderation make all the difference between diabetes being in the background of his day or being his primary focus.

This is why we keep the alerts tighter than what is medically suggested. Because while those ranges may be safe, they aren't ideal for Jonathan for how he wants to feel and function. And those high and low feelings don't immediately go away once he gets back into range. Depending on how long and how severe, it can take hours or even the whole day for him to regain his equilibrium.

JONATHAN

When I was admitted into the hospital because of my T1D onset, I didn't understand the significance of my blood sugar being around 360 mg/dL. Some people with T1D live their lives in that range calling it a high blood sugar, when in reality that is an extremely high daily reading. I mean if it is a number that sent me to the hospital, it is probably not a good number to have on a regular basis.

When I first started wearing the Dexcom, I left the ranges at the default settings which were pretty wide. I think the top of the range is 400 mg/dL. My mom wanted me to set tighter ranges, but I didn't want the alerts to go off while I was in class. I didn't want to draw attention to myself. At my high school, many teachers require students to put their phones in a pocket organizer on the classroom door so they aren't distracted during class. However, since I had accommodations to keep my phone with me to monitor my blood sugar, I was able to keep it in my pocket. I would do my best to go into classes with a steady line on the Dexcom, but despite my best efforts I occasionally had to take out my phone to check my blood sugar and treat a high or low.

However, I realized that by not having tighter alerts, I was setting myself up for emergencies, which would draw more attention to me than the buzzing in my pocket. So I tightened my alert range to the levels where I could function well and it still allowed me to get in front of a potential low or an extreme high.

Sometimes I do get out of range intentionally. As weird as that sounds, having too low of a blood sugar level can put a person at risk of not having enough energy or falling to a dangerous low during activities. Of course you still need to have a range gap of where you want to be. For me, I try to stay between 80-140 mg/dL during the day. However, when I workout, I usually start my training around 140-160 mg/dL. I try to never go above that because if my blood sugar goes too high, it can produce negative effects on the body and can make me feel tired, sluggish, and make me lose my drive to be active.

Success comes with proper nutrition and not a fatty or sugary snack. Sugar burns very fast and thus results in a quick high followed by a crashing low. This leaves you with zero energy and confidence. I achieve my desired high with something like a protein shake (consisting of thirty carbs), protein bar (consisting of twenty carbs), Greek yogurt with berries, granola, and oats or honey (forty carbs) or sometimes a complete meal before my workout. The decision regarding which one to do is based on different criteria such as my current blood sugar, what I have already eaten for the day, what workout I am doing, etc. This way I have real nutrition and complex carbs that take longer to break down. With this plan, I am able to start my workout around 150 mg/dL and at the end of my two-hour training be at a nice 100 mg/dL.

Sometimes, I am not in a position to have a good meal or snack before an activity. So I always carry quick acting foods with me. When I participate in any activity: paintball, working out, bike riding, hiking, etc. I have protein bars, juice boxes, and glucose tablets/gel packets on hand. Each of these items in some combination creates a quick rise and a longer-lasting effect in my system, helping me stay in range even when I am busy living.

My mom wants me to set my alerts even tighter, but right now I don't think I need to do that. Maybe when I move into a full-time career where my days are more consistent. I have so much activity in my life that I believe my current targeted range of 80-140 mg/dL is fine.

TECHNOLOGY: DEALING WITH PRICKS, PUMPS AND MONITORS

MICHELE

Technology has truly been a gamechanger in the type 1 diabetes (T1D) community. We recognized that right away and chose to use it to help Jonathan best manage this autoimmune disease.

As an adjunct communications college professor in the early 2000s, I taught students how to design marketing materials using desktop publishing software. I would tell my students that just because they buy a hammer and some nails, it doesn't qualify them to build a house. The same was true for design. They had to understand design basics and what the computer was doing for them in order to create something of value. So we spent one-third of the semester learning about design elements such as typography, white space, images, and contrast before they turned on the computers and built their portfolio materials digitally.

I took that same approach with the T1D technology. I recognize that I can't use it blindly and expect it to solve all of Jonathan's glucose concerns. I couldn't just turn it on and hope for the best. It really comes down to garbage in, garbage out. In other words, we have to use it correctly and input the right calculations into the technology for it to appropriately respond to Jonathan's lifestyle – and we can only do that if we understand what his body needs and how the technology uses the information we provide.

Additionally, should any technology fail and we have to temporarily revert back to multiple daily injections (MDI), knowing the correct basal, insulin-to-carb ratios and correction factors will help Jonathan stay better in range.

Most doctors want to set up their patients for long-term success by ensuring they know how to manage their T1D before the doctor writes a prescription for an insulin pump. Often patients wait anywhere from six months to a year. Jonathan's endocrinologist agreed to move us to an insulin pump much quicker than other patients because we proved to her that we understood the basics of diabetic management and we had a good handle on his personal numbers and how to keep him in range. So if you are wanting to move to an insulin pump sooner, the best advice I can give is to learn what works for you so that you can demonstrate that knowledge to your endocrinologist.

There are many technological solutions out there, so again it comes down to what works best for your family, lifestyle, and goals. You will want to ensure you choose what is covered by your health insurance. Sometimes the health insurance covers multiple options and sometimes there is only one choice. Also remember to choose technology that interacts with each other for the best results and management.

Besides the immediate benefits Jonathan gets by using this technology, his endocrinologist is also able to gather months' worth of data that enables her to give better guidance during Jonathan's quarterly appointments. We link our Dexcom and Omnipod with the Glooko.com website and it tracks and captures the data automatically from the devices. The data can be reviewed in many different ways. The below data is one of Jonathan's thirty day summary reports.

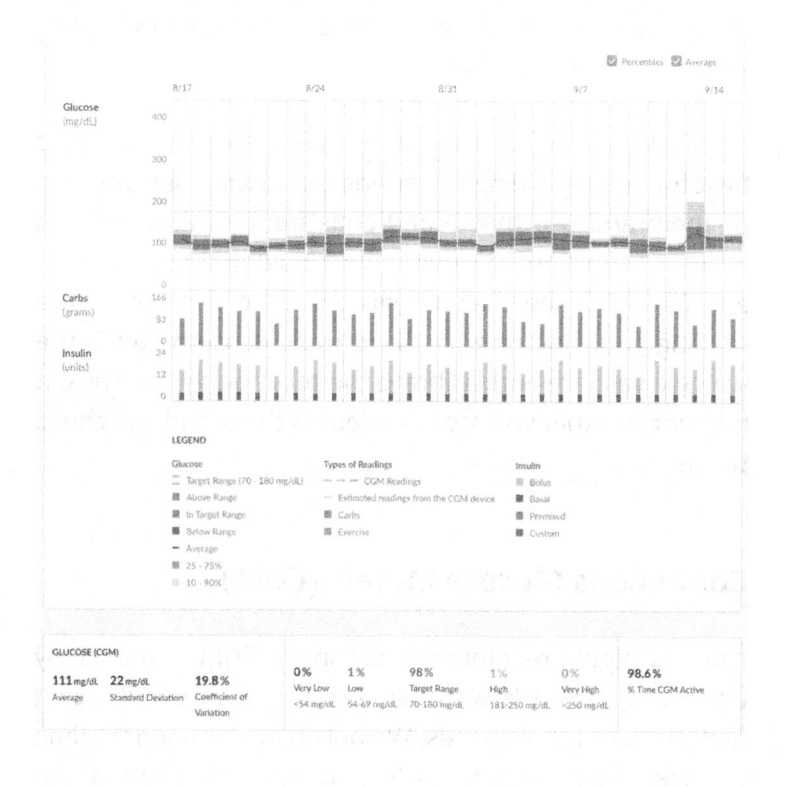

Glucose Meters

The biggest thing I learned about glucose meters is that they are not all the same. We received one from the hospital, one from our health insurance and another one in the mail. They were all different brands and the test strips and lancets did not transfer between them. We did a test to see if they all read the same result from the same blood sample. Guess what. They didn't. In fact, each time we tested them, the variance differed. Not too drastic, but enough to be noticeable.

My best recommendation is to find the one that works best for you regarding finger pricks and then buy a couple of them and use that brand consistently. Also, you can bring it with you to your endocrinologist appointment and check to see that it registers close enough to the reading your doctor gets. Since the glucose meter is the way we validate and calibrate the technology readings, it is important that you are confident in the brand you chose to use.

Continuous Glucose Meters (CGM)

I would highly recommend getting a CGM immediately upon diagnosis. We were blind to his glucose levels that first week of his diagnosis. We only had a moment in time to make judgments regarding his care throughout the day. I didn't know if he was trending down or trending up when I calculated his correction factors. I had no idea how the foods he consumed were truly affecting him. It was hard for me to determine how best to help him with how he was feeling because I didn't have a clearer picture of what was happening inside his body.

Additionally, only checking his glucose level at school before lunch or marching band isn't enough to keep him medically safe. There are so many factors that affect glucose and so many unplanned moments at school that unexpected highs and lows are bound to happen on a regular basis when managing via MDI.

Having a CGM helps mitigate the highs and catch the lows before they become dangerous. It helps you learn how different foods and activities affect the glucose level so that you can make more informed decisions. It also provides peace of mind when your teenager is out and about, at school or participating in extracurricular activities and events.

Our endocrinologist was very helpful with this. I ran across CGMs in my research. There are several different options out there. We went with the Dexcom G6 because it has the most accurate rating of what is currently available. His doctor sent in the prescription and Jonathan started wearing his CGM three days after his hospital discharge. This device is attached to Jonathan's body in roughly the same areas he can give himself insulin shots. A tiny sensor is inserted under the skin and measures the glucose level in the interstitial fluid. He changes his CGM every ten days.

We have been very happy with it.

- It makes a huge difference in being able to understand a more complete picture of what is happening and how best to determine Jonathan's personal numbers to manage his T1D.

- It allows us to see beyond the carb effects and into the other elements that impact glucose levels including when he is sick, active, tired and more.
- We are able to understand how pre-boluses, extended boluses and temp basal are working and what adjustments need to be made.
- It alerts us to highs and lows so that we can address them before they develop into an urgent situation. We have ours set well within his recommended medical glucose range which allows us to keep him in better range and feeling his best. I have one sound for when he is higher than our desired range, a different sound when he is low and an annoying one for his urgent low notifications. I have found it is best to change these sounds periodically so that I don't get accustomed to them and start sleeping through them.
- We no longer have to do a finger prick around 3 am, so Jonathan gets a better night's sleep.
- It reduces the amount of finger pricks we had to do overall. This was especially meaningful for Jonathan who, as a drummer, needed to not have bruised and tender fingers.
- It is compatible with the Apple Watch, giving quick access to current glucose levels.

We still calibrate it after the first twenty-four hours and then again if it seems wonky – especially now that we are looping it with the Omnipod 5 and it is used to determine the automated insulin delivery. We also still do finger pricks to validate crazy highs or lows – or when Jonathan feels different than what it is reading.

Jonathan is able to track his Dexcom readings on his phone and I can use the "Follow" app to help him monitor his levels. Yes, at first you will be glued to this app. The first few weeks I checked it all the time which is crazy because I had the alerts set very tight to notify me if his glucose was trending even slightly high or low. I didn't need to check it unless it beeped at me, but I did. I told myself I was analyzing. I was conducting research. Truthfully, I was a petrified mom. I am way better now and often forget about it until it beeps – unless, of course, he is trying something new and we are actively watching his glucose response.

A couple of things to note. Sometimes we get false readings:

- Compression lows when he is sleeping because he has rolled onto the CGM device. This looks like a quick, inconceivable drop out of nowhere on the graph. It corrects once he rolls off of it. If this happens, check to see if it instantly corrects itself before treating for the low. Some people cushion the Dexcom to help prevent this from happening, but this is not something we do.

- False highs or skipped readings when he is dehydrated. The skipped readings look like the Dexcom is drunk and the tracking line is not aligned to the rest of the dots on the screen. Jonathan drinks a glass of water to see if the number drops and does a finger prick if it stays constant before administering a correction bolus.

- Jumpy readings during the first twenty-four hours while it is "warming up" on the body. Some people put the new sensor on their bodies a day before they take the old sensor off. This is called "soaking" and it is said it helps the transmitter be more accurate. (The new sensor isn't registered on the receiver/phone until they are ready to move the transmitter over.) We have not tried this.

- Consistent bad reads if we try to calibrate when the arrow isn't horizontal. If we are treating a potential high or low and the arrow is slightly angled or vertical, we finger prick and, if off, we treat appropriately and wait until it evens out to finger prick again and calibrate. Waiting to calibrate is highly recommended if you have just bolused, exercised or eaten due to expected fluctuation in glucose levels that come with those activities.

- Consistent bad reads if we try to calibrate the CGM for a variance more than 20 mg/dl. In this instance, we make sure the arrow is horizontal and then we do multiple calibrations. So for instance, if Jonathan's glucose meter says 70 mg/dl and the CGM says 110 mg/dl, we would calibrate to 90 mg/dl, then immediately again to 70 mg/dl. This process enables more accurate readings after a significant disparity between the numbers.

We are excited about the Dexcom G7 because it is tinier, takes only thirty minutes to warm up, and is better calibrated. However, they are still working to pair it with the Omnipod 5. Given this, we will probably wait for them to fix all the bugs before we transition to it.

Insulin Pumps

Moving from MDI to an insulin pump made a significant difference for us because it acts more like the pancreas. It allows us to adjust insulin based on Jonathan's needs throughout the day more successfully. We did have to make some minor adjustments in Jonathan's insulin-to-carb ratios and correction factors from what we had calculated in MDI – mainly because we could vary his basal settings throughout the day and no longer had to compensate for the steadiness of long-acting insulin. There are a couple of different types of pumps and they all have features that should be considered before deciding which one to use. We chose the Omnipod because Jonathan didn't want to worry about tubing given how active he is.

With the Omnipod we are able to do things like:

- Set temporary basal levels for activities or illnesses.
- Program different basal levels throughout the day.
- Program multiple manual modes so we can switch Jonathan's insulin delivery with one step vs having to reconfigure his daily needs (*Below the Carb Surface* covers Jonathan's different modes).
- Create extended boluses to tackle even the toughest combinations of foods and keep him from experiencing a rollercoaster day.
- Give micro and correction boluses without dealing with multiple injections.

Using an insulin pump also gives Jonathan more flexibility in public and when he is out with his friends. No longer does he have to worry about carrying needles and insulin or trying to privately bolus for a meal when he is dining out. And no longer does he have to worry about whether the insulin he is carrying is getting too hot or too cold depending on the weather outside. We started with the Eros version then switched to the Dash. When we heard about the Omnipod 5 (O5) being able to "loop" with the Dexcom, we switched to that model as soon as it was covered by our health insurance.

He carries a separate Personal Diabetes Manager (PDM) device with him since the O5 doesn't work with the iPhone – but he doesn't mind it too much. Also many of the above bullets are still programmed into the O5 PDM and can be used in manual mode, but for the most part, the algorithm does its own thing. It took us a while to teach the algorithm how to help Jonathan stay in range. Basically, the algorithm predicts where his glucose level will be an hour in the future and adjusts his insulin delivery every five minutes. The goal for the system is that about half of the total insulin delivered in a day comes from basal insulin and the other half from boluses. We had to be diligent whenever his glucose level trended above our desired range to manually administer a bolus so that the algorithm knew how aggressive Jonathan wants to be with staying close to his targeted glucose level.

The first couple of months were frustrating because his glucose trends weren't as controlled as when we had him on the Dash. On the Dash, Jonathan spent most of his time in range between 80-120 mg/dL. With the O5, the lowest programmable target is 110 mg/dL, so his glucose level ran higher on average even though his A1C still stayed in the 5% range. There were also times when the O5 didn't know what to do because for the most part Jonathan had steady glucose trends. Leta me explain. One day at 4 am, he experienced an extreme low – but he told me he was on top of it and not to worry. So I went back to bed. About an hour later I woke up to a rising glucose that was nearing 300 mg/dL. I checked his PDM and there was an orange line on the graph. A red line means the O5 has stopped giving insulin because it is expecting a low glucose level in the near future. However, an orange line means that the O5 isn't giving insulin because it has reached the maximum bolus it usually gives during this timeframe. So we had to administer a bolus to tell the algorithm that it is okay to give more insulin at that time of day to keep him in range. He coasted down into range and the O5 went back to administering insulin as needed.

Instead of freaking out in the moment, I used what I had learned to correct what was happening. Later that day when we were all awake, Jonathan explained what he had done to treat the low and agreed he had over treated it. At the time, he was tired and thought the O5 would take care of any high. But since he is usually around 100 mg/dL in the early mornings and the O5 usually gives a minimal bolus during that time frame, it didn't "want" to give the insulin that was needed to correct the rising glucose level "until it knew it was okay to do that". Overall, we are pretty happy with how the O5 provides automated insulin delivery.

For both Jonathan's Omnipod and Dexcom we don't worry about weather or activity. He does everything wearing both. Depending on the activity (such as swimming), we may need to check the Dexcom periodically to ensure it is sending the readings to his phone. We don't worry about being out in the cold or Texas heat – except we are careful not to get sunscreen or insect repellent on either of the devices as these products can crack the plastic and cause the devices to malfunction.

We are also careful to move the devices around a lot so that he doesn't develop scar tissue. Scar tissue makes it harder for that area to absorb insulin and it can negatively impact glucose readings. Because he is into weightlifting, he doesn't have as much fat on his arms and legs, so he rotates both devices around the front and back of his abdomen.

Some people have reported issues with the adhesives. Either they are extremely sensitive or the devices don't stay on well due to oily skin. Many people spray an antihistamine on the skin before applying the devices to avoid skin irritation and rashes. There are also all types of overlays to help keep the devices on the skin and help prevent accidental removal. These come in clear, solid colors, colorful patterns and fun themes. Dexcom will also send a package of clear overlays every month. You just request them on their website every thirty days. We used a couple of waterproof overlays the first summer when Jonathan was at the beach or pool. But unless he is snorkeling, we realized he doesn't stay in the water long enough to really need them. Also, Jonathan usually wears a rash guard which helps protect both devices.

Regarding removing the adhesive, he uses an alcohol wipe when needed. There are several different solutions on Amazon, but we have found an alcohol wipe usually does the trick and costs a lot less. Jonathan does use medicated lotions on previous sites to help his body repair faster and keep the skin from drying out. He also massages the area to avoid developing scar tissue. He does this with his hands or with a handheld deep tissue massage gun set to low.

On occasion we have had some mishaps and had to replace the Dexcom or Omnipod before it was time. In these instances, the companies have been great about sending us a replacement.

One time he called me at school to say he accidently ripped off his Dexcom. Nothing spectacular, just moving through busy hallways and it got caught on a door handle. It ripped enough that it needed to be changed.

Another time, we noticed that every time he bolused for a meal he would drop immediately to low glucose levels. We were having a hard time keeping him in range even when he wasn't eating. The highest he tracked for three days was in the upper 70s and his Omnipod was set on the "extremely active" mode which delivered the minimum amount possible. When it was time to change out the Omnipod, he thankfully decided to take it off while showering. I say thankfully because as soon as he did, blood started spewing out of the site. He had hit a vein when he put it on and the insulin was being delivered directly into his bloodstream causing him to have extreme lows. If that happens again, we will change out the pod immediately.

As I am typing this, we experienced another sleepless night thanks to T1D. Jonathan had a jazz concert as part of a university fundraising event, so he waited to change out his Dexcom before heading to bed and forgot to change

Michele Segura

his Omnipod setting to manual vs automated. He had also experienced a low so he had about thirty uncovered carbs. He was in the low 100s but slowing trending up. I suggested he give himself a correction to steady the line before he went to bed – but he forgot. So for two hours, I had "no reading" alerts and then for the rest of the night I was alerted that his glucose level was high. Usually, if the Dexcom reading is under 200 mg/dL for the first couple of hours after "going live", I do nothing because I know that the Dexcom is probably off and needs to be calibrated. I learned this through trial and error of waking him up to treat what I thought was a high, only to discover the reading was way off and Jonathan was comfortably in range. Most often by morning it has corrected itself or narrowed the gap. However, in the wee hours of the morning his Dexcom was showing a steady 270 mg/dL. I checked his PDM. The Dexcom connection was spinning/searching so the Omnipod wasn't registering the reading. When there is no reading, the O5 falls back to the last known reading and dispenses accordingly or gives the minimum bolus programmed. Well, it hadn't been giving him any insulin for several hours since it was on auto and had paused administering insulin because of Jonathan's low before he changed out his Dexcom.

The perfect storm.

Jonathan woke up and did a finger prick. His glucose level was about 70 points better than the Dexcom reading, but he was still high. He connected the two systems, gave himself a correction bolus and went back to bed. My best advice:

- Change the CGM when you are steady, not planning to eat any meals or be active and are still awake during the warmup process. Sometimes that means we change it out a few hours before it expires. Usually we target after his evening shower – meaning Jonathan takes off the Dexcom, showers, then puts on a new one.

- If you have a looping system, it is best to switch the pump to a manual program during this time. If you are steady and at a level you are happy with, then the looping works well. But otherwise, we have found it is best to switch to manual and then back to automated once the Dexcom is online.

Apps

There are a couple dozen apps in the Apple App Store that offer assistance in everything from carb counting, glucose tracking, and bolus calculation estimates. They also trend glucose over weeks, months, and even years with detailed dashboards and easy reporting that could be shared with your medical team. Some offer reminders and alerts by integrating with your CGM. Several of the apps are designed by others with T1D.

As I mentioned earlier, we used Sugarmate for a long time while we were gathering intel on how to best help Jonathan navigate his T1D. When we used the Sugarmate app, I had it set to call my phone if Jonathan went low. This can be a lifesaver especially if you forget to turn your phone off silent mode. I have done this. Sugarmate came through and called my phone number until I answered. Several parents of college students post that they use Sugarmate to help alert them to an urgent low so they can reach out to roommates, campus security or EMS if their sons/daughters are not responding to texts and calls.

It is a good idea to test a few of the apps and see if any can help you with your insulin management. Again it's all based on individual needs, lifestyles, and desired outcomes. For some, keeping up with the extra data entries may be too much at first and that is okay. It is important for you to know that these resources are available and can make T1D management easier for you.

Other Helpers

The number of solutions coming out to help people with T1D is very encouraging. We have a SugarPixel to help Jonathan wake up to his low or high notification alerts. It looks like an old digital desk clock and displays the glucose reading and trend arrow. It also alerts those present when he is out of his desired range. So even if Jonathan sleeps through his phone alerts or forgets to change from silent mode, the SugarPixel will wake him up. Some people program Alexa, Siri or Google to notify them. And there is also this nightlight device called Glowcose that changes colors depending on your glucose level. It is exciting to see products and solutions come to market that are focused on making monitoring easier and saving those with T1D from life-threatening lows.

AirTags and Tiles are also good options to help ensure PDMs, phones and other critical supplies don't get lost. These are small devices that can attach to anything and will even play a sound to help you locate them. Many people use these on their PDMs since the PDMs don't have a built-in tracking system.

JONATHAN

I am really glad that the technology for managing T1D continues to get better. I honestly can't imagine having to think about everything I need to think about without the assistance of my Dexcom and Omnipod.

I hated having to be woken up in the middle of the night to check my blood sugar level. It often left me tired in the morning. And the idea of going to school without having a sense of what was going on with my body made me nervous. So I was glad my mom was able to get a prescription for the Dexcom before I went back to school.

Wearing the Dexcom helps me understand how my body is responding to what I am doing so that I can continue to make improvements in managing my T1D. At first, I had a love/ hate relationship with the Dexcom CGM. I remember the first couple of times I put it on my body it hurt. But only for a couple of minutes. I think part of the pain was because it was new and I expected it to hurt. Now, I would say the initial insertion stings more than anything else.

I also struggled with the idea that my entire family could look at my blood sugar numbers whenever they wanted. It doesn't really bother me anymore because I realize my family doesn't look at it as much as I thought they did. Well, except my mom did at first. But now, she is a lot better because the diagnosis isn't so new anymore and we are more comfortable with managing my blood sugar.

Wearing an insulin pump has helped me feel more like a normal person. I hated having to excuse myself at a restaurant and go into a bathroom to inject myself with a needle. Anyone who has ever been in a men's bathroom knows how disgusting it can be. My brother, Zach, would tell me to bolus at my seat like other T1Ds do, but I hated the idea of people watching me stab myself. While Zach is very outgoing and would probably start a whole conversation with the stranger watching him, I am more reserved and avoid drawing attention to myself when at all possible. I was also afraid of needles when I was first diagnosed and was concerned I would nick someone by accident. So I preferred to be in an enclosed area and not around other people.

Because of this I didn't like eating out and it was hard for me to hang out with my friends for too long for fear of getting hungry around them and having to bolus for my food. With the Omnipod, I just pull out my PDM and bolus. Most of my friends think I am checking something on my phone so my diabetes management goes completely unnoticed.

The only issue I have is placement for both of these devices. Because I am lean, I don't have much fat around my arms and thighs. It is uncomfortable and can be dangerous to insert the Omnipod into a muscle. I tried placing the CGM on my upper arm. It bent the cannula and I had to remove the CGM within a day. It left a bruise on my arm for a week. So I wear both my Dexcom and Omnipod around my midsection where I try to maintain enough fatty tissue to wear these devices and have them work well. This consists of my stomach area, sides, and back.

I also have to be mindful about rotating them so I don't build up scar tissue or putting them on a spot where one was recently because it can irritate my skin. I try to aim for spots where I can grab at least a pinch of skin. I have placed these devices on myself where I thought "this is a good place, right here on my side" only to find out that it was very painful and deciding "never again".

I do wish my CGM and insulin pump were smaller and that they lasted longer than ten and three days. Luckily I know the Dexcom G7 should make a difference in the size. My current CGM isn't that bad, but the sticky adhesive base does have a very wide perimeter. I chose the Omnipod for my pump because it doesn't have any tubing, so I don't have to worry about that with my active lifestyle. I have snagged both on things such as door handles, seatbelts, and more. I am now more aware of my surroundings in those situations.

SCHOOL AND WORK ACCOMMODATIONS

MICHELE

Education is important. There are more than enough distractions to hinder students from learning what they need to know. We want to ensure diabetes management isn't one of them for Jonathan.

Fortunately Jonathan was diagnosed at the beginning of a semester, so he didn't miss too many assignments. Since my husband is in education, I knew we would need to create a 504 plan for Jonathan. These are legally required school plans to ensure students with mental, physical or medical disabilities receive accommodations to enable their academic success in a safe learning environment. The majority of school districts require a 504 plan before being allowed to return to school mainly to cover their liabilities. Most often it necessitates a medical plan from your endocrinologist. The diabetic educator from our endocrinologist's office was a great resource for this. She was responsive and eventually added a stipulation to the medical plan that we could make our own changes to Jonathan's care and no longer needed a signed plan from the doctor's office. This meant I didn't have to get a new medical plan each time we adjusted his insulin-to-carb ratio or other treatments.

Any school who tells you that type 1 diabetes (T1D) doesn't qualify for a 504 plan needs to be educated, as T1D falls within the protection of the Americans with Disabilities Act. But don't let that classification concern you. We do not see Jonathan as disabled, but we do want him to have the accommodations he deserves to help him succeed while managing his T1D.

In all honesty, most school administrators, staff and nurses will have little idea how to help you unless there are other students with T1D in the school with educated caregivers who have previously demanded proper accommodations. You most likely are setting the groundwork for how the school manages students with T1D going forward. Based on our experience, you need to advocate for everything you want and you need to help your teenager become more comfortable advocating for him/herself.

Jonathan and I also discussed how private he wanted to be about his new medical diagnosis. Some teenagers like to share and be an educator to other students. Others, like my son, choose to keep their diagnosis more private (at least at the beginning). I remember what he said to me as we discussed going back to school.

"I don't want you to tell anyone about me being diagnosed with T1D."

"Well, I need to tell the administrators, the nurse and your teachers at a minimum. Also your band director needs to know because of marching season."

"I don't want people to know that my body quit on me. I don't want to be treated differently. Like I can't do something. Or that my achievements are only because people feel sorry for me." He replied.
"Your body didn't quit on you. It was attacked and it fought the best it could, and you only lost your pancreas' ability to produce insulin and glucagon. It can happen to anyone."
"I still don't want you to say anything."
"Okay. I do, however, think you should tell one of your friends. Especially on the drum line. Just in case you are having a low during a performance and need help."
"I'll think about it. But for now, I just want to be Jonathan. Not Jonathan who also has T1D. Just Jonathan. Okay?"
"Okay... for now."

Additionally, we talked about communication. We discussed what was expected in response time, how to communicate the need for insulin, treating lows, etc. Since he wanted to be more private with his T1D, we developed a code for texts. When Jonathan was younger, he had a couple Tamagotchi toys. For those who don't remember this fad, these were digital creatures the size of a keychain that the owner was challenged to hatch and grow into an adult. This involved responding to the beeps and actions happening on the screen. If the owner didn't respond appropriately, the creature would die. So, we jokingly called his Personal Diabetes Manager (PDM) device his Tamagotchi and I would text things like, "feed your Tamagotchi" when he was running high and needed to give himself some insulin. And if he was starting to go high or low – he would text us, "I'm good" which meant he was aware and taking care of it so we didn't need to worry or bombard him with texts.

Michele Segura

High School Accommodations

We contacted the school to develop Jonathan's 504 plan in partnership with the school nurse and counselors. When contacting the school, it is best to say something like, "My son's health has changed and I am seeking educational 504 accommodations for his new chronic medical condition" and then also follow up in an email for documentation purposes. Using buzz words like "accommodations" trigger certain due diligence (at least in the state of Texas) that school administrators must address.

Developing a strong 504 plan requires that you spell out everything – and modify the 504 plan as you learn more and things change. So when we developed Jonathan's 504 plan, we included every accommodation we wanted him to be able to use, even though he only used about half of them on a regular basis.

We considered these accommodations for Jonathan's 504 plan:

- Whether or not we want him to manage his diabetes or if he needs more help/intervention with the school nurse and/or teachers.
- If he wants the right to go to the nurse at any time including before the end of a class to prepare for lunch and PE.
- If he wants the right to use the restroom as needed and have access to water at all times.
- That he was allowed to have snacks during class for glucose lows (younger kids often have a snack box in

each room, older students usually carry snacks with them).

- That he has the right to correct for highs and he has the right to go to the bathroom or nurse for this vs doing it in the classroom if using multiple daily injections (MDI); once he transitioned to an insulin pump it was very easy to do this at his desk.

- Since he used a continuous glucose monitor (CGM) and insulin pump, that he is allowed to always have his phone and PDM on him to monitor his diabetes.

- Whether or not he wants testing and assignment accommodations for high/low glucose levels – like pausing/stopping a test, extra time to turn in assignments, making up missed work, etc.

- That for anything diabetes related (extreme highs/lows and endocrinology appointments) he receives excused absences and tardies and that these did not count against his total missed time allowed for graduation requirements.

- When to notify parents of high/low, behavior concerns (refusal to eat or take insulin), pump malfunctions, etc.

- Teacher awareness and training of the T1D indicators for low glucose and how to respond.

- Whether or not we want the nurse, trained staff, or parent to attend field trips, off campus events and overnight trips. If you include this, write out a checklist of necessary items to take when leaving the school premises.

- Since Jonathan was older and brought his lunch to school every day, we didn't request carb counts for school food and notices of any special treats (birthdays, holidays, special events), but this is common for younger students.

As far as educating teachers, other students, school staff, substitutes, care providers, and bus drivers, there are some great templates I found on sites like *beyondtype1.org*, *breakthrought1d.org*, and *t1dmodsquad.org* that can be customized for individual needs. Remember to also inform extracurricular teachers and sport coaches about your teenager's needs and your expectations. Finally, ask the nurse for a cell phone number so you can exchange texts throughout the day.

The school asked us to provide extra supplies like insulin, needles, glucose monitor kit, extra insulin pumps, and an emergency treatment for extreme lows. We provided some of these things to the nurse and Jonathan elected to keep the rest on him. At first, we had a special bag I purchased for his diabetic supplies. But once his diabetes management became more routine, he reserved a pocket in his backpack for them. Now, he keeps them in a crossbody bag that he wears when he is out and about.

As Jonathan was in high school and very dependable, we gave him more control. Was he nervous? Absolutely. Did we make mistakes the first few weeks? Sure. But nothing was too bad; the mistakes were small and quickly fixed.

Originally, Jonathan went to the nurse's office to have her help him count carbs and confirm the correct bolus. But after a few weeks, he was much more confident to bolus on his own. He still went to the nurse when he felt out of range or needed to call me for a replacement because his pod or CGM malfunctioned.

When the time came for Jonathan to return to school after his diagnosis I was an anxious mess. It reminded me of the first couple of weeks after he got his driver's license and started driving himself everywhere. Honestly, the whole situation scared me. We were both still learning, but I knew I was more educated than the school staff on how to handle his T1D. He could have stayed home and switched over to eLearning but he was ready to go back. He missed his friends, he missed being in classes, and he missed band. And I had to let him go.

I reminded him not to drive if his glucose was under 100 mg/dL and trending down – that he needed to correct for any lows and have a steady arrow when he was behind the wheel. *(Not only for his own safety reasons, but also because this can be used against him if he was ever in an accident.)* I gave it to God, packed his supplies for his backpack, the supplies for the nurse and sent him on his way.

I texted him reminders way too often those first couple of weeks. I jumped the gun and called the nurse when he was low and trending down or when he didn't respond fast enough to my texts. I raised a smart, disciplined guy, but my momma bear instincts often forgot that during most of his first semester back. It's because everything was a new experience for us and we didn't have a reference for how to prepare or how to best respond. Almost 100% of the time, he was managing fine. Most of the time he thanked me, a few times he got frustrated with me. But he always knew I had his best interest in mind.

One afternoon right before a scheduled pep rally, his glucose started to plummet out of nowhere. I was on a conference call when the low alerts started going off. He was at 70 mg/dL. Then 60 mg/dL. Then 55 mg/dL with a straight arrow going down. In a matter of fifteen minutes he was at an urgent low. I knew he was getting ready for the pep rally and would be somewhere on campus. Not in a class. Not easy to find. As the drumline captain, he led the student parade through the school and into the gym. The adrenaline he usually felt wasn't kicking in this time. I excused myself from the meeting and texted him with no response.

54.
Still no response.
52.
I called. No response.
My heart was racing. I called the nurse.
55.
She answered. "Yes, he was just here, did a finger prick, downed two juice boxes, and left for the pep rally."
60.
"Yes, he had his drum with him and seemed fine. He had it under control enough that I didn't need him to stay."
67.
"I'm fine can't talk pep rally" came his text across my phone.
75.
No more alerts. He was steady in the 90s for the rest of the afternoon and his usual protein afternoon snack jumped him into the low 100s for marching band practice.

I did not emotionally recover as fast as his glucose level did. But the incident provided an opportunity for Jonathan to prove he was on top of it and managed it well enough that it didn't interfere with his plans. We talked when he got home. We don't know what caused the drop. He hadn't bolused or eaten anything for a couple of hours and he ate his usual lunch. His morning routine was normal and he was in range before the drop. Maybe his pancreas decided to participate that afternoon since Jonathan was still honeymooning.

Higher Education Accommodations

The easiest way to qualify for higher education accommodations is to continue the 504 plan through the end of the senior year in high school, regardless of whether all of the accommodations are still needed.

We requested the high school counselor send Jonathan's 504 accommodations to the College Board so that he could have accommodations while taking his SAT and ACT tests. The College Board decides what accommodations, if any, they will grant – and they did grant the right to have his phone in the room (although at the proctor's desk), to pause his time to treat an unstable glucose level, and to have necessary supplies/snacks on hand.

As soon as Jonathan was accepted to his university of choice, we sent his final 504 plan, a copy of the College Board approved accommodations and a letter from Jonathan's endocrinologist to the school's Student Disabilities Services Center (SDSC) requesting accommodations. In her letter, our doctor outlined the following requested accommodations for Jonathan's college courses:

- Ability to consume food or drink during class if needed to treat low blood sugar levels.
- Ability to perform diabetes care in class.
- Ability to "stop the clock" or reschedule exams to treat a high or low blood sugar during an exam which can affect cognitive functioning.
- Ability to bring medical supplies into testing facilities including, but not limited to, a continuous glucose monitor, insulin pump, phone and other supplies.
- Ability to take exams in a monitored remote setting (testing center) so as not to distract other students while treating blood sugars.
- Ability to have priority class registration to allow the best possibility of a consistent schedule semester to semester which can improve diabetes management and allow times for meals to keep blood sugars stable and attend medical appointments.

It is important to do this as soon as possible because it can take several weeks to complete the approval process. There is usually an SDSC committee that reviews and approves all the requests for accommodations. We were told upfront that Jonathan may or may not receive every accommodation that we requested. If any accommodation wasn't approved, we could appeal with additional information. There are pre-meetings, clarification meetings, approval meetings, confirmation meetings and appeal meetings that must get scheduled around everyone's calendars. And each meeting requires specific completed forms before they can be processed.

A delay could mean that the semester starts before accommodations have been awarded. At Jonathan's university, professors cannot grant any accommodations until the accommodations are approved by the SDSC and then, the approved accommodations only apply to classes/work going forward and are not applicable to prior assignments and tests.

Jonathan received all the accommodations he requested. He was fortunate to have an SDSC advocate who understands T1D.

What is different with higher education institutes is that they work directly with the adult students and not the parents. It doesn't matter who pays the bills. The university only speaks with enrolled students because they are adults. All emails go to the student's school account. All forms must be signed by the student. This is why it is so important to get your teenager comfortable with self-advocating.

Once accommodations have been approved it becomes a semester-by-semester cycle. The student provides the SDSC with a list of classes for that semester. The SDSC sends an email to each professor letting them know of the student's approved accommodations. Then it is up to the student to meet with each professor to work through what the accommodations mean for that class. And this process repeats every semester.

If your teenager decides to live on campus, it is also important to discuss a communication and action plan with the roommate, Resident Assistant and Resident Hall Coordinator, as well as notifying the campus police should you need to contact them in an emergency.

Work Accommodations

Many people struggle with whether or not they should tell their employers about their T1D. I believe you don't need to tell anyone about it until after you get the job – unless it could directly impact your ability to do the job's primary responsibilities. However, once you are employed, your direct supervisor and probably at least one co-worker should be aware in case you need help treating an unexpected low. This is true even if you are a remote employee.

If you do decide to request accommodations, ensure you get the approval in writing – this can be accomplished by sending a follow up email to summarize the verbal agreements that were made. As T1D is a medical condition, it falls under the protection of the Americans with Disabilities Act and the privacy of the Health Insurance Portability and Accountability Act (HIPAA). You can't be denied an opportunity because of your T1D as long as you can show you are able to perform the essential job functions.

This is another reason why we strive for good management and control. If you have good control over your glucose, your T1D is less of an issue and therefore, it reduces the opportunity for you to be discriminated against because of it. I have read several online posts where people have issues at work because their CGM alerts are constantly going off and disturbing their coworkers. Most coworkers don't understand the employee's "sounds" are medical alerts and there isn't a requirement to tell them. However, when I read these posts, my immediate thought is how can we help that person with T1D level out their glucose levels so they are not getting alerts all day, every day.

JONATHAN

I enjoyed going back to school because it helped me somewhat put diabetes in the background of my day. Most days.

When I did MDI, I would leave class to go to the nurse when I needed to bolus for lunch, give myself a correction bolus, or check my blood sugar. The teachers already knew that if I got up, it was because I was headed to the nurse for something diabetes-related, so they never said anything or made a big deal about it. I guess most students thought I was headed to the bathroom or leaving early for one of the numerous band-related performances that popped up all the time.

I did have issues with a few substitutes who did not read their class notes to know that I had accommodations. Most often I would quietly explain to them that I have a medical condition with 504 accommodations and needed my phone with me or needed to go to the nurse. That usually ended any dispute. However, one time a substitute refused to believe that I could keep my phone. She told me to surrender it immediately or she would call the office. Thankfully I am very comfortable advocating for myself. I told her to call the office or even the nurse, but that I was not giving up my phone. The office confirmed my 504 accommodations and the substitute left me alone after that.

Because my body was finally on the road back to being healthy and consuming the energy I was putting into it, I carried around snacks with me all the time at school. My mom also made my lunch every day so that I didn't have to worry about having an unexpected high sugar level while in class. Even during senior lunch, where we were allowed to leave the school, I would take my lunch and eat my own food at whatever fast-food restaurant my friend group decided to go to that day. When other students questioned me as to why I was always eating or why I always brought my own lunch, I simply told them I wanted to be a bodybuilder and I was bulking and watching what I ate.

While we were still working to determine my numbers and basal settings, I often had nights where I ran very low. This caused me to be up for an hour or two before falling back to sleep just in time for my morning alarm to jolt me out of bed. I would wake up groggy, still very tired and often with a headache. My mom would let the school know I was going to be tardy due to T1D, allowing me to get an extra hour of sleep before starting my day – which made a world of difference.

Luckily my first class was Honors band and my band director was very understanding. He knew I already had my music memorized and that I was on top of my responsibilities as the percussion captain, so my tardiness didn't impact my ability to perform.

However as a student leader in the band, I didn't want my peers to see me as weak because of my diabetes, so I never told them about my life-altering diagnosis and how it affected me. This resulted in some of the other students thinking I had become lackadaisical about my commitment to band during that first semester after being diagnosed. Which was the furthest thing from the truth. They had no idea how many hours I practiced and the additional hours I spent helping younger percussionists learn their instruments. They also didn't know how hard I worked to stay on point while managing a high or low blood sugar during summer band, football games and marching performances. Fortunately, I was able to remain a strong role model through my senior year because of my dedication to the band and its underclassmen.

When I started college I had to submit paperwork to get accommodations. It is quite a detailed process, so I am glad I did most of it over the summer. There were several zoom calls that I dialed into to explain my needs and hear what the committee determined. The first semester I was a little lost about knowing exactly what to do to get my accommodations in each of my classes. Fortunately, my advocate worked with me and my professors to help me resolve everything.

Getting a part-time job was a little nerve racking because I wasn't sure how cooperative employers and co-workers would be with me possibly needing breaks to manage my blood sugar. Luckily my first job was at a private gym and it had a great environment. I worked there evenings after school and sometimes on the weekends. I was able to get along with everyone and my employer let me take care of my blood sugar whenever I needed. He had seen me successfully working out for more than six months in that same gym so he knew I was managing my T1D really well. This set a positive outlook for me about what I wanted to look for in my future career.

However I had the opposite experience with my second part-time job. During my first semester in college, I was selected for a strength coach internship with the university's athletic department. I worked with the Olympic style teams to help them prepare for games and recover from injuries. I really enjoyed being around the athletes and helping people build their strength in the gym. I needed to be very quick and ready at a moment's notice to be called on while working and even on breaks. But the coach I reported to didn't like me pausing to manage my T1D. She was only a few years older than me and didn't have experience as a people manager. This made for a stressful work environment.

My day started at 5 am with the internship and ended at 10 pm with my job at the gym. Not to mention my college courses, homework and jazz practices and performances in between. This schedule began to impact my body. Waking up early was hard on me because, as I mentioned before, not getting enough sleep makes the body more resistant to insulin. Stress does the same. While I maintained good blood sugar levels throughout the internship, I decided to cut it short because my boss and I couldn't see eye-to-eye regarding how I managed my T1D needs.

My current part-time job is working as an instructor for a local taekwondo's afterschool and summer camp programs. This includes picking up students from school, teaching classes, helping with homework, chaperoning field trips, and managing student discipline. The dojo master is a fantastic boss and offered me the position after being a student of his for several months. This job aligns with my desire to help people live healthier lives and my coworkers have my back at all times.

When looking for a job, above everything else, find an employer who works with you. We all deserve to find employment and a community/environment that supports our needs.

CREATING A T1D ZONE

MICHELE

I'm pretty sure I've already mentioned that I am a type A person. Yes, a type A caregiver for a type 1 teenager – what a combination. An organized house keeps me sane. So when I received Jonathan's first ninety day order of diabetic supplies I knew I needed to create an organization strategy. I wanted to ensure he had easy access and usage, we were using products according to their expiration dates (first in, first out rule), and I knew what we had in stock and what needed to be ordered.

I also wanted Jonathan to feel as if he had a space that was his own and that he didn't need to be ashamed or embarrassed about having type 1 diabetes (T1D). It was part of his life and we would make a place for it in our home.

What worked for us was taking over a side of our kitchen's island. Jonathan has a set of three drawers where we store his quick access items, as well as one cabinet where all his excess supplies are kept. Everyone in our family is aware that his supplies are stored as follows:

- Top drawer has everything he needs to check his glucose and treat lows (to include his Baqsimi for a severe low glucose level), as well as his current bottle of insulin. I do keep it in an insulin vial protective case in case it is dropped (ordered off of Amazon).

- Second drawer has "next use" Omnipods and Dexcom supplies and overlays so he can take care of his technology changes as needed and without help.

- Bottom drawer has a container for used needles, syringes, and lancets (I use an empty protein mix container and then screw the lid on and dispose of it when it is full – this follows our current local disposal guidelines), along with extra cotton swabs, alcohol wipes, replacement supplies for his glucose meter as well as a backup glucose meter.

- In the cabinet, I store the extra pods, transmitters, sensors, and glucose tablets. I have a small book in there where I have copies of all his prescriptions. We get a peel off label each time with his prescriptions, so I stick those on the pages and I have quick access to all that information. I also have a basket with supplies we use when traveling and a laminated index card with a list of current items I pack (insulin, pods, transmitters, etc.) to help me remember everything.

- In the pantry we have a section dedicated to lower carb and sugar-free foods, protein bars, and fast-acting glucose options. This helps ensure he is grabbing the right food when he is making his own meals or heading out for the day.

- We purchased a small refrigerator that I put in our utility room – which is near Jonathan's bedroom.

This is where we store his supply of insulin vials and backup long-acting and short-acting insulin pens. I keep a thermometer in there to ensure the insulin stays at an optimal temperature. We also store juice boxes in there for quick access. This allows us to have the needed space in our refrigerator, as well as gives him privacy from house guests grabbing something out of the fridge.

An idea I have seen that looks like it would work well is an over-the-door plastic shoe storage organizer. I think if Jonathan ever decides to move the supplies to his bathroom, that is what we would most likely do for him in that space – to ensure we keep everything dry. Others have dedicated a utility or hall closet with labeled baskets. Do what works for your family.

Some questions to consider: Does your teenager need reminding or help administering insulin and placing the Omnipod and Dexcom devices? Does s/he want more privacy? Do you need to keep the supplies away from curious little sibling hands or frequent guests?

Planning for Emergencies

Something to think about is what you will do in case of an emergency. If you were faced with a weather, fire or other urgent situation, do you have an evacuation plan that includes taking enough supplies with you? What supplies will you take? Can you easily get to them so that if you have to take shelter somewhere else for an extended period of time, you can still manage your T1D needs?

Michele Segura

I didn't think much about this until a month into Jonathan's diagnosis when we were hit by the 2021 Texas Snowpocalypse. For those who don't live in South Texas, let's just say snow is one of those things we hear about each year but rarely experience. That February, it snowed not once, but twice in a matter of a few days. We had close to eight inches on the ground at our house alone. It was fun at first until the Texas utilities infrastructure began to fail. At first there was no electricity for many and then no water, since there was no electricity to keep the water pumps going. It took about a week to get everything back online and working properly. Fortunately for us, we were only without running water – but I realized then that I needed to plan for the possibility of losing electricity so I could protect the precious insulin we had on hand and charge our phones and Jonathan's Personal Diabetes Manager (PDM) device so we could stay aware of his glucose levels.

We invested in a solar generator and an electric cooler in case of emergencies. This is also helpful when going camping or spending an extended amount of time outside and away from current day conveniences. The coolers come in all sizes and price ranges. The electric cooler can be plugged into a car, a generator, or an outlet and is a perfect safe haven for unopened insulin if we lose power or are out in the hot Texas sun for days. When Jonathan moves out, he will take these with him so he will continue to have the backup he needs to stay on top of his diabetic management.

JONATHAN

I do appreciate having my own space with all my supplies. My mom made it feel normal for us to have everything I need to manage my T1D. My stuff is out of sight, but it is convenient to me. It now seems like that space has always been for my T1D supplies even though I have only had T1D for a short time.

As a teenage guy, I admit I am not always organized as much as I should be. But knowing I only have one or two spots where I can find everything I need that is diabetes related helps me be more successful at self-managing this autoimmune disease.

I feel the same about the food in the pantry. It's nice to have everything together so I can quickly find what I want. While I am at an age where I easily identify what is in the pantry for me, if you have younger children, I recommend putting their food on a lower shelf so they don't accidently grab what we refer to in our household as "fully loaded" foods.

The idea of having an emergency plan and backup solution is important. Most of us plan for daily low blood sugar emergencies when we are out and about, but taking time to ensure you can grab the T1D supplies you need for a long-term emergency situation is something everyone should consider. I realize I probably shouldn't expect emergency shelters to have insulin, diabetic supplies, glucose, and T1D technology to support me.

OUR CONSTANT TRAVEL COMPANION

MICHELE

We love to travel so it is important to me that Jonathan feels confident being away from home for extended periods of time. How we pack and prepare for our trips has come from trial and error and acknowledging lessons learned.

On a weekend beach trip, the constant water and activities created the need for more frequent pod changes even when using the waterproof adhesive covers. Then because of bad weather and road closures, we had to stay another day than what we planned. We had enough supplies to get us home, but if the roads had been closed longer, we may have run out.

Another time we were visiting my brother and his family for the day and as Jonathan went to bolus for his meal, he accidentally deactivated his pod. I didn't bring any supplies because, you know, it was just for the day and Jonathan had just put on a new pod that morning before we left. Thankfully we called the local CVS and explained the situation to the pharmacist. She reviewed Jonathan's prescription file and was able to fill an emergency prescription for us so that we could enjoy the holiday visit vs leaving immediately for the two-hour ride home. Now, even if we are traveling for the day, I carry an extra Omnipod and insulin with me.

When we were traveling overseas the PDM had trouble registering the time zone changes correctly. Because of this, the PDM kept deactivating the pods and we went through three pods in less than twenty-four hours. After a call to the Omnipod help desk, we reset the PDM and didn't have any more issues on that trip. Thankfully because we planned to snorkel several days, I had packed one pod for each day we were traveling as well as an extra vial of insulin.

I'd rather have more than enough supplies with me, then have to cut a trip short or spend time chasing down a way to get extra supplies locally.

Now when we pack for trips, we always plan for one more round of T1D supplies than we expect we will need (not just one more day of supplies). For instance, if we are going to be away for five days and Jonathan has on a new Omnipod and Dexcom, I pack three Omnipods and one Dexcom set. If either is due to expire in the next twenty-four hours, I pack an additional one. I include enough insulin (in bottle protectors) to fill all the Omnipods I am taking, as well as his glucose meter and supplies. If we are going to be gone for an extended time, I also take back up insulin pens with the needle tops in case we have technology issues and must resort to using multiple daily injections (MDI). Since insulin is good for thirty days unrefrigerated, I do not worry about trying to keep the insulin cold – I just ensure that the insulin is protected and that it stays at room temperature. I also always pack his severe low glucose treatment (currently Baqsimi).

We also pack plenty of snacks that I know work for him to forego having to deal with unpredictable high glucose levels. Depending on how long we plan to be gone, I might even carry a sleeve of Jonathan's favorite low carb buns with me for those easy access sandwiches or burgers in airports and along the highways. A simple bread replacement such as this often makes for a hassle-free meal experience.

Additionally, I ensure I pack a healthy supply of glucose tablets and gel packets, electrolytes and vitamins. For the electrolytes, I use the individual serving packets. With the vitamins and supplements, I use a daily pill storage container so he can easily keep track of whether or not he has taken them.

Airports and Flying

Jonathan's T1D supplies travel with us and are not packed away. I've never had any issues going through TSA with them. We have all medical and low glucose supplies in a separate bag and identify it as a "medical necessities bag". No one has ever questioned me about it or asked me to open the bag for inspection. I think part of this may be because we are enrolled in the TSA PreCheck program. If you travel often and can participate in this program, I highly recommend it to avoid having to unpack your carry-on bags through security. We completed our TSA applications at the local Staples store and were approved in less than two weeks. The membership lasts for five years and costs about eighty dollars. Some people find it helpful to have a note from their doctor indicating what medical necessities are needed when traveling. I've heard this is important documentation to have for some countries, but so far this has not been required for the countries we visited.

Jonathan also has no trouble getting through security scanners with his Omnipod and Dexcom on his body. At first he would tell the TSA agent he has type 1 diabetes and is wearing an insulin pump and continuous glucose monitor (we avoid acronyms in situations like this). They would do a micro pat down and send him on his way. But lately, he walks through without saying anything and so far it hasn't been an issue.

We usually do not check in any bags. If we did, I would use that space to pack more of the snacks and food we might not be able to find during our travels, but I would continue to keep his medical supplies as a carry-on bag.

A couple of lessons we have learned while flying. Altitude and cabin pressure can affect the insulin pump. One time we flew to Denver and there was a storm in the area. As we began our descent, Jonathan noticed that suddenly his glucose level was dropping fast. We flagged down the flight attendant for an apple juice and Jonathan drank the entire can. He stopped declining but stayed low. We exited the plane and did a glucose meter check. Yes, his Dexcom was reading correctly. Jonathan consumed an additional thirty more carbs before he leveled off near 100 mg/dL. I couldn't understand what happened until I looked at the Personal Diabetes Manager (PDM) and realized that the cabin pressure had sucked eight units of insulin out of his Omnipod. Thinking about a partially filled bottle of water and how it gets sucked in with the cabin pressure – this makes sense. This doesn't happen every time we fly. We only seem to have this issue when we have flown through a mountainous area. Note, this was not discussed in the initial Omnipod education literature, but after receiving feedback from many travelers, Omnipod has updated their safety page to include this notice.

So now, depending on where we are traveling, we may either suspend insulin delivery or snack throughout the ride without covering those carbs and allow his glucose to run a little higher than usual to mitigate an unexpected urgent low. I know some people who have said they actually remove their insulin pumps or disconnect them (if they have tubing) when they are flying because of this concern.

We have learned the best way to minimize the cabin pressure issue while traveling is to take direct flights and avoid multiple takeoffs and landings. We started with shorter flights when he was first diagnosed to help us navigate this new normal. The longest flight we have been on since he was diagnosed is nine hours overseas. We didn't have any issues on the flight – just ensured he was well hydrated the entire day. One thing to keep in mind is to update the time zone on the insulin pump once you land so that when it connects with your phone it remains in sync. Otherwise, the pump will deactivate

Another issue is that while Jonathan continues to receive his continuous glucose monitor (CGM) readings, I do not get them in the "Follow" app while in airplane mode. This means that if he decides to sleep, he turns up the sound on his phone so that all of us can hear if a low glucose alarm goes off.

Hotels and Lodging

When we get to where we are going, the first thing we do is identify a T1D zone in the new space. This is important so that Jonathan can continue to self-manage and everyone knows where the supplies are in case of an emergency. Usually, we keep his supplies in the medical bag either on a designated table, counter, or in a drawer. Another thing I do is scope out the surrounding area to determine where the nearest pharmacy is just in case we need it.

Road Trips

Road trips surprised me. I didn't expect car rides to impact him, but I soon learned they did. A few months after Jonathan was diagnosed, we drove to Dallas for a bass fishing tournament. This was our first time away from home since Jonathan's diagnosis. We were still doing MDI and overall Jonathan was consistently in the 70-150 mg/dL range. The trip distance is about three hundred miles, but with the traffic and construction that is ever present on IH35 North in Texas it took us almost eight hours to arrive. About an hour and a half into the trip, I noticed on my Dexcom Follow app that Jonathan's glucose was creeping up. He hadn't eaten anything and was asleep in the back seat. By the time we arrived in Dallas, he was steadily in the upper 100s. We added additional insulin based on his correction factor when he ate, but he still didn't level out into our preferred glucose range. In the middle of the night, I received an alert that he was nearing 200 mg/dL.

Out of nowhere our T1D management method had blown up. We were careful with what he ate and even increased his bolus amounts since we were eating out, but the trip had gotten the better of his glucose level. After a few correction boluses overnight, he was back in range and the rest of the trip went fine until we headed home. Same trend. I theorized that it must be the long car ride because he isn't moving around and active. Also, he wasn't drinking much water during the ride which impacted his insulin delivery.

So a few weeks later, when we drove to the Texas coast about three hours away to do some saltwater fishing, I tested a temp basal setting during the trip and Jonathan had much better glucose levels the entire time. We continued to dial in what worked best for him. Now, when traveling for more than an hour by car, Jonathan increases his basal setting by +30% for the duration of the ride and ensures he drinks water to avoid dealing with a stubborn high glucose level.

Environmental Impacts

It is important to keep in mind that the environment can impact glucose levels. We often notice that during the first week or two of weather variations and seasonal changes

Jonathan experiences unexpected glucose levels that cause him to pump extra insulin or grab more glucose tablets. His glucose evens out once his body adapts, but sometimes the fluctuation can be rough.

Because of this, we keep the following in mind when traveling:

- We use the first twenty four hours to see how Jonathan's body is responding to insulin and food in the new environment before we jump into any extreme activities.

- Hot weather can cause him to have lower glucose levels, so he is prepared to need less insulin and potentially experience faster lows during activities.

- Cold weather can cause him to have higher glucose levels, so he is prepared to need more daily insulin and have insulin on board during activities.

- Higher altitudes can mess with his T1D in a couple of different ways. It can increase his glucose levels requiring extra insulin to combat stubborn highs. It can increase insulin resistance so he may need more insulin to cover the carbs he eats. Jonathan is also prone to altitude sickness, which feels a lot like having low glucose levels, so we are more mindful to watch his glucose until he adjusts. Sticking with low carb meal choices in higher altitudes makes this much easier to manage.

Some people with T1D experience just the opposite from Jonathan – highs in hot weather, lows in cold weather. And some do not sense any environmental impacts on their bodies. However the environment impacts you, it is important to know that it can.

Medical Alert IDs

These don't seem like much, but they can make a difference in a severe low or an accident where the individual with T1D is unresponsive. A few first responders I know say that they do look for medical alert IDs as part of the initial assessment when arriving on scene. There are a ton of choices and designs out there to fit everyone's tastes. I've even seen some adults who have tattooed themselves as T1Ds – but I am told first responders don't look at tattoos. Originally, Jonathan opted for a T1D bracelet that he wore; but that interfered with his drumming. So we ordered a T1D pendant that he added to his cross necklace. It is discrete but enough to alert first responders that he is insulin dependent.

JONATHAN

Growing up, my family traveled all the time. My mom believes that the best gifts are experiences. Instead of gifts for special occasions, we travel. So I was excited, but also a little hesitant about what traveling with T1D would look like. My mom said it just means we need to pack an extra bag. And that is how we approached our first couple of trips.

Airports are a pain because it is very difficult to find good low carb food choices. The medical bag we pack has my extra pods, sensors, insulin and other T1D supplies, as well as snacks that work for me. I also carry a low carb hamburger bun or two that I can trust not to jack with my blood sugar. A lot of the time, our only quick options are burgers or sandwiches. With the extra buns we carry, I swap the bread out and then I can enjoy my meal without the spike.

When we first started traveling after I was diagnosed, we would spend time between our flights exploring the airports we frequented with the goal of finding restaurants where we could order low carb options. Then we stuck with these "go to" choices every time we went through those airports. Sometimes our best option is a salad bar where I order double protein. I bolus minimally upfront for these meals and then follow up with a bolus to assist with the protein rise that comes later.

I tried other options and had to deal with undesired high blood sugar for a good duration of the travel day. In these situations, we would try to walk it off before we had to board the next plane and sit for hours. I remember one time when we were in Atlanta. Our flight was out of the D concourse, but my blood sugar was trending toward 200 mg/dL. We had about an hour before we were scheduled to board our next flight. So my mom and I went down to the train level and walked all the way to the T concourse and back before heading to our departure gate. That leveled me out around 100 mg/dL and allowed me to enjoy the rest of the travel day.

I used to put my Omnipod on weekend mode when I flew because I was so inactive throughout the day. But after experiencing an extreme low while flying because the air pressure sucked out insulin from the pump, I leave the pod in automated mode and check it regularly. I have also learned to not put on a new Dexcom sensor right before we travel. There is no need to add that additional stress of waiting for the sensor to warm up and calibrate while we are en route to our destination.

Car travel is a little trickier. I have to know how long I am going to be in the car to determine if I can ride in automated mode or if I need to increase the basal rate. Basically, I realize that I have to compensate for the fact that I am not moving around as much as I normally do and I am also not drinking as much water because I don't want to be the reason we stop. I try to ensure I get in a decent workout the day before we travel so that I have good insulin sensitivity on the days I am stuck in the car.

When we get to where we are headed, my mom creates a T1D zone for me. There I find all my diabetic supplies, snacks, electrolytes, vitamins, etc. that enable me to continue to successfully self-manage my T1D even away from home. This has brought me much comfort and I am more enthusiastic about traveling again.

RECONFIRMING YOUR NUMBERS OVER TIME

Just as our bodies change as we age, so does our type 1 diabetes (T1D) needs. It is important to reconfirm your basal, insulin-to-carb ratios and correction factors periodically or when there is a significant change in your health or lifestyle.

Most veterans of T1Ds recommend doing this at least once or twice a year. Even if you use an automated looping system like the Omnipod 5 and Dexcom combination, you still should check your numbers periodically to help you with your diabetes management, as well as prepare you if your technology fails and you have to resort to multiple daily injections (MDI) for a period of time. Of course there are the normal considerations – don't do it when you're sick, before/after unusual activity, not while drinking alcohol and no recent hypoglycemia events. Your endocrinologist should be able to provide you with the detailed steps to do this. But I wanted to offer a brief introduction and explanation in the book.

Basal Setting

The first step is to get your basal settings dialed in to keep you in your desired glucose range. This is critical if you want the rest of your testing to be accurate. It is easiest to do this by dividing the testing into a couple of days. Basically you fast for six to eight hours at a time and track your insulin delivery against the glucose levels on the continuous glucose monitor (CGM), making notes of any fluctuation and adjusting your settings either higher or lower.

Insulin-to-carb Ratios

The second step is to ensure you have the right insulin-to-carb ratio(s). There are a lot of step-by-step guides online to help you do this, but basically you:

- Ensure you are starting in a good glucose range and haven't eaten or bolused in several hours so as not to skew the results.
- Pick something to eat that is familiar, simple, and low-fat to get the best clarity. You must know the true carb amount for this to be accurate.
- Bolus as you normally would for the food and then eat and track the results. I like this tracking chart template from diabetesnet.com. It is a great visual plus it has all the data fields you need to track. Another reason I like it is because sometimes we get so fixated on trying to achieve a super straight glucose line all day, every day, that we forget it is normal to have a glucose rise

after eating. Our goal should be to mimic that normal rise, not erase it.

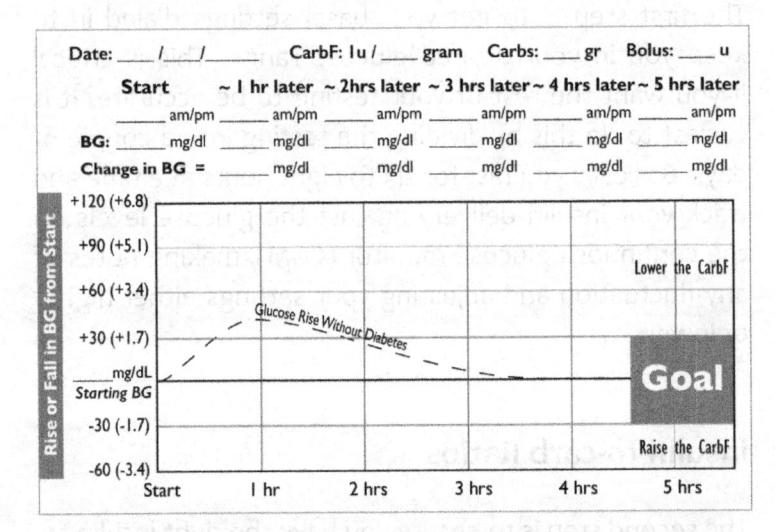

Date: __/__/__	CarbF: 1u / __ gram	Carbs: __ gr	Bolus: __ u
Start	~1 hr later ~2hrs later ~3 hrs later ~4 hrs later ~5 hrs later		
__ am/pm	__ am/pm __ am/pm __ am/pm __ am/pm __ am/pm		
BG: __ mg/dl	__ mg/dl __ mg/dl __ mg/dl __ mg/dl __ mg/dl		
Change in BG =	__ mg/dl __ mg/dl __ mg/dl __ mg/dl __ mg/dl		

Rise or Fall in BG from Start

+120 (+6.8)
+90 (+5.1)
+60 (+3.4) — Lower the CarbF
+30 (+1.7) — Glucose Rise Without Diabetes
__ mg/dL Starting BG — **Goal**
-30 (-1.7)
-60 (-3.4) — Raise the CarbF

Start | 1 hr | 2 hrs | 3 hrs | 4 hrs | 5 hrs

Used with permission; additional charts and information can be found in the 6th Edition of Pumping Insulin by John Walsh and Ruth Roberts.

- Based on the results you either tighten or loosen the ratio.
- The standard is to retest two more times with the same amount of carbs to determine if you have the right ratio.
- If you have different insulin-to-carb ratios throughout the day, you should test each one of them during that time frame.

Correction Factor

Finally you confirm your correction factor. This has to be done when your blood sugar is higher than normal and steady, because you are testing how much one unit of insulin will lower your blood sugar. You'll want to do this with no extra insulin on board from a previous bolus. I've been told it can be done two ways:

- First method: Correct as normal and see where you end up after three to four hours. If you are not back to your target, then you may need to tighten your factor (so 1:40 vs. 1:50). If you have passed your target, then you may need to loosen your factor (so 1:50 vs. 1:40).

- Second method: Give one unit of insulin and see how far the glucose comes down after three to four hours. That change indicates what your correction factor should be. (So if your glucose is at 150 mg/dL and one unit of insulin brings it down to 125 mg/dL, your correction factor is 1:25.)

Again, standards recommend testing this three times to ensure consistent results.

If you are uncomfortable with making your own adjustments, do this right before your next endocrinologist appointment and share your findings with your doctor so that s/he or the diabetic educator can work with you to adjust your settings.

FINDING YOUR VILLAGE

MICHELE

Veterans of type 1 diabetes (T1D) and experienced caregivers often say, "Welcome to the club that no one wants to join. We are sorry you are here, but we will support you the best we can." And so far, it is true. There is an outpouring of help from those who are living with T1D daily. Everyone wants everyone to be effective with every part of their diabetic management. It is a community that openly shares what they know so others can achieve success too. It's an amazing group of strong and determined individuals who are united in helping each other live healthier lives.

I have found that the biggest debate in the T1D community is around diet. Should you choose low carb meals or eat whatever you want? Should you eat three regular meals or several small meals throughout the day to spread out the carbs and minimize the bolus amount for each meal? Even then, there is a level of respect for each other's choices and tips on how to successfully bolus for the food that others avoid.

This is the type of support that makes it easier to navigate how to best manage T1D throughout your life. The broader community will be there to support you, but you also need your individual coaches and cheerleaders to help you achieve success.

Doctor and Medical Office

It goes without saying, you have to have a good relationship with your endocrinologist. We were lucky enough to get a fantastic one. A doctor who listens to our questions (and we always have a written list of topics to discuss during Jonathan's appointments), engages in meaningful conversations, and is willing to adjust treatment solutions to achieve the outcomes we want.

We have access to a doctor on call twenty-four hours a day and direct lines to the office's diabetes educator and the insulin pump adviser. Jonathan's doctor helped us obtain a continuous glucose monitor (CGM) quickly after diagnosis. She prescribed him an insulin pump when we were ready. She ensures we have the supplies we need to safely get us through the ninety day prescription coverage and enables us to have the long-acting and short-acting pens for backup purposes. And she gave us guidance when we started to explore participating in a T1D study. She is also responsive to patient portal emails and after hour phone calls. Jonathan's doctor even wrote a letter to the university's Student Disabilities Services Center to help him get approval for his learning accommodations while attending college.

When Jonathan turned eighteen we worked with his pediatric endocrinologist to recommend an adult endocrinologist who treats their patients in a similar way.

If this doesn't describe your endocrinologist, find a new one. While you only see your endocrinologist three to four times a year, that doctor and the office staff are your lifelines to manage everything from school/work accommodations to prescriptions for supplies.

Healthcare Insurance

You may not think of your healthcare insurance company as part of your village, but it can be. Nowadays, these companies have realized that the best way to improve their profitability and reputation/brand is to proactively help their members with chronic conditions stay healthy. Otherwise those individuals wind up in the emergency room with expensive claims. So many health insurance companies provide additional services and support for people with chronic conditions.

The best course of action is to reach out to your health insurance company and talk through all the diabetic coverages, programs and support that it offers. Not only for the necessary supplies and technology you plan to use, but also for nutritional and mental wellness needs. Whether or not you intend to use them right away, it is good to know what is available to you and your family so that you can make the best choices when you are ready.

Regarding supplies and technology, find out what the preferred coverage is for insulin pumps, CGMs, insulin brands and types, glucose meters, etc. Usually the preferred brands and models will be cheaper in regard to copays. Also, know what is covered through pharmacy and what is covered through durable medical equipment (DME). Often there are different co-pays and coverage depending on how the insulin pumps and CGMS are classified. It can also mean that you have to order the supplies differently. Sometimes you can get the supplies from a local retail pharmacy and sometimes you have to use a specialty or pharmacy mail order which means you need to plan ahead to account for shipping and potential delivery delays.

Knowing this information as soon as possible is important if you have to get your endocrinologist to write an appeal or get a prior authorization (PA) for the specific supplies you use that aren't covered by your insurance. It is good to know this ahead of needing the supplies as it can take weeks for all the approvals to go through even when they are marked as urgent.

Coverage can change year-to-year, if you switch to a different insurance company, and sometimes even if you use the same insurance company but sign up for a different plan, so you should investigate this every annual enrollment period and every time you change your plan. Additionally, consider setting up your supplies for automatic refills and prescription renewals and set the parameters for the soonest a refill can happen. By doing this, you don't have to worry about missing an important refill and often it will enable you to have a few days of overlapping supplies in case you use more insulin than usual, have a leaky insulin pump, or a faulty CGM sensor or transmitter.

The health insurance we had when Jonathan was first diagnosed proactively reached out to us upon leaving the hospital. We were assigned a case manager, a nurse, a dietician and a social worker. Now we had a network of people to help us navigate our healthcare coverage and T1D needs. Not solely for Jonathan, but for the family as well. The case manager helped us navigate coverage and needs. He put in calls for us to other internal departments regarding decision delays, coverage understanding and even worked with our doctor's office to get the necessary paperwork we needed to get approvals. He also connected us with programs that offered free glucose meters and supplies. The nurse called us to ensure we understood all of Jonathan's prescriptions and asked if we needed help in learning how to better administer them. The dietician talked with us about our food choices. The social worker informed us of counseling coverage and provided a list of support groups in the area.

I changed jobs about a year into Jonathan's diagnosis. It was a little more challenging this time. During my open enrollment, I had to call back multiple times to determine which insurance plan had the right coverage for us. Every time I called I got a different answer. It wasn't until the fifth call when I was thankfully connected with someone who had T1D in their family. They were able to provide me with answers to all the coverage questions I needed to make the right choice for our family. Once we were customers, the insurance company was great – but again, their open enrollment reps weren't trained to answer the questions we had.

And that happens all too often. Sadly, the customer service reps who answer the phone calls cannot be trained for every scenario and disease, especially when the companies make annual coverage changes to their plans. Frequently the companies are also behind in updating their call center scripts to enable these employees to point customers in the right direction for these types of services. Don't give up. Ask to speak with a supervisor or manager. Ask to be connected to the chronic care or diabetic care team. Even if you get to a representative who usually works with type 2 members, they will know enough about coverage to help you out. Sometimes, sending an email or opening a chat through the health insurance company's member online portal will successfully route you to the right team for help.

When thinking about insurance coverage, it really comes down to three things for me:

- Are Jonathan's doctors in the network?
- Does the insurance cover his preferred insulin and medical devices, where do they fall in coverage (Pharmacy or DME) and at what formulary tier (higher tiers have higher copays)? This helps me determine what I can expect to pay out of pocket above the monthly premiums.
- Deductibles and Maximum out-of-pocket (MOOP): what is the most I have to pay that year before insurance kicks in at 100%? I compare the plans based

on a combination of MOOP, deductible, copays and the amount of annual premium I pay. With Jonathan's medical needs, he may be able to be covered 100% much quicker in the year thereby reducing my overall medical expenses.

T1D Support Groups

I strongly recommend finding support groups even if it is only online. There are quite a few Facebook support groups and they range from general T1D groups to location specific (such as Texas), specific diets (like low carb) and technology being used (as in Omnipod, Tslim, Medtronics). Our local Breakthrough T1D chapter is pretty active and I have started volunteering at fundraisers and participating in events. I have met many wonderful T1D community individuals this way. Unfortunately, it lacks the young adult participation that would be great for Jonathan.

I also follow some of the companies and nonprofit organizations that support T1D to stay in the know with current guidance, research, products and sometimes local social events and fundraisers.

Now that Jonathan is more comfortable sharing his journey with others, he checked to see if there was a T1D support group on his college campus, but there is not. He is working with the Student Disabilities Services Center and The Diabetes Link to establish a chapter on his campus. The Diabetes Link is an organization that focuses on three issues student experience at college: "the lack of a support group, the spontaneity of college life that can lead to poor diabetic management decisions and the desire to be normal which may result in neglecting diabetic needs". There are some helpful tips about college life at thediabeteslink.org to include topical resources, interviews with other college students, and links to scholarships and jobs specifically in the T1D community.

Caregiver Support

I have talked in detail about Jonathan, but I want to pause and mention how important it is for the caregiver to have a support network as well. If not for yourself, for the loved ones who need you. Your support network may come from a spouse, relatives, friends, neighbors, or grown children – but you need to find it.

We are rather private people and don't post our lives on social media, so while I follow many pages, I don't post much in terms of seeking support. But the people behind the posts I read are my village, even if they don't know me personally. They bring me comfort that there are others out there fighting the same fight and crushing it. Because of them, I know we can do it too.

Honestly, I was able to move through my grief of his diagnosis pretty quickly. That is who I am. I recognize that many see me as "a hard ass" – my family jokes about it all the time. But really it is just that I prefer to focus on moving forward and solving for what is ahead. As the high school Band Booster president, I used to tell the parent leadership team that we don't have to do something because that's the way it has always been done. Traditions are great, but we need to do what works for the band program now and what the students in this year's band want and need. So if what we have been doing in the past no longer provides value, let's do something that does. And that is really how I approach life in general. So for Jonathan, I need to focus on what works for him here and now, not what was envisioned for him years ago. I know God has a purpose for Jonathan. My job as his mother is to help him be the person he was born to be.

I have some amazing friends who don't know much about T1D, but they bring me balance by allowing me to focus on other topics when we get together. We grab a bite to eat, attend social events in our town, and participate in hobbies like painting classes. A few of them live far away, but we talk and text regularly. They help me focus on me and remind me of who I am as a person. When I choose to bring up T1D, they listen, provide an outsider's perspective and help me think out loud in a way that can bring clarity I don't find on my own.

My extended family doesn't understand the complexities of T1D, so while they ask, "how's it going," it's hard to have deep discussions. They all want the best for Jonathan and care deeply about his health and long-term success. They engage him in conversations about T1D if he brings it up. And they are thoughtful to plan for low carb options when we get together for meals. But because he was diagnosed as a teenager, they have never had to help manage care for him so the reality of the autoimmune disease is secondhand.

My husband is terrified he will do something wrong. Instead of learning how to help manage T1D correctly, he chooses to leave the caregiving entirely to me. He's great in other aspects. He has taken on more household chores and volunteers to walk with Jonathan to combat a high glucose level if I am busy. But he has no idea what to do when an alert goes off or what advice to give Jonathan for how to bolus for a meal.

And honestly, being the sole T1D caregiver as we navigated our new normal has been hard. I work full-time including travel and I volunteer extensively. As a night owl, I really hadn't thought much about the need for sleep most of my life. As for stress, my blood pressure is a consistent 117 over 72 so I thought I was handling everything well. But the broken sleep night after night and the 24/7 worrying began to have its toll on me.

During the first year of Jonathan's diagnosis, I gained twenty pounds due to stress, lack of sleep and overall not taking care of myself because I was so focused on setting up Jonathan for success. At one point I ran my tank so close to empty that I came down with the flu, strep and bronchitis at the same time. Even with two rounds of steroids and antibiotics, it took almost eight weeks for me to return to my usual healthy self. But me being sick didn't mean Jonathan's needs went away. Through this I realized that by keeping myself healthy, I am better prepared to help Jonathan.

I am thankful that my older son, Zachery, helps me where he can. He moved back home before Jonathan's diagnosis to finish college locally and has been involved in Jonathan's journey. Occasionally, he travels with us to Boston for the clinical trial Jonathan elected to participate in with the Joslin Diabetes Center. He has listened to me enough that he can support Jonathan when they go out together in terms of meals and correction boluses and treating lows. He is also great in talking with Jonathan and reinforcing the advice and tips that I have shared. I know Jonathan appreciates having someone else to talk with besides me.

We all need a village – some bigger than others. That is okay. Find your village. Fill it with coaches and cheerleaders who can assist and remind you that you are not alone in any aspect of this journey. And recognize that while your villages may intertwine, your village and your teenager's village may be filled with different people.

JONATHAN

It took me a while to decide who of my high school classmates I wanted to tell that I was diagnosed with T1D because, let's face it, many people that age aren't mature. Because I have a great relationship with my older brother, I have always been mature for my age. Luckily, this attracted mature people to my close friend group who I decided were the only students I wanted to tell. These friends take my situation seriously in a way that they can help me if needed, but also treat me like I don't have T1D. My advice is to find and confide in people like that.

When explaining my diagnosis to my close friend group, I realized that sharing this with everyone in school wasn't for me. Mainly because I didn't want to explain the difference between type 1 and type 2 diabetes to everyone I told and everyone they told. At least not yet.

I often feel alone with my diabetes because I seldom see others who also have T1D. I do recognize that some people, like me, don't show it. And there is not a specific way to identify someone with T1D from their appearance unless you spot a CGM or pump. Because of this I do get excited if I see a fellow T1D and try to connect with them. I am working with my university and The Diabetes Link to create a T1D chapter on campus, so I am hoping to make friends with other Type 1 Warriors.

As great as my family is about helping me I sometimes get annoyed with them. Don't get me wrong, I love my family and have a very close relationship with them. But it's not fair that during the time in my life when I am becoming more independent, I still have constant reminders of how to live my life. My mom constantly reminds me to bolus and my dad and brother text me when I am out of normal blood sugar range "just to let me know". This bothers me because I am so attuned to my body that I know when my blood sugar is changing or about to change up to thirty minutes before it happens.

Even as I started my first semester in college, they kept looking out for me and offering to help me before I asked for it. Now I know how that sounds. But truthfully I wanted them to look out for me more indirectly.

One night over dinner, I had a conversation with them and explained that I want to be able to fail. I felt that I understood the basics well enough that I needed to ensure I could handle my life on my own before I was actually on my own. And that means I may run higher than my mom prefers before correcting. It also means that I didn't want them to immediately come into my room at night to help me correct a low blood sugar level. If they see me addressing it, let me do it on my own. Now if it has been more than fifteen minutes or if I am not waking up to a severe low, then, of course, offer assistance. But other than that, they have to be okay if I am not running in range as consistently as I normally do.

So now, I pretty much manage T1D on my own from a daily perspective. My family is always ready to take a walk with me if I ask. My mom is always available to talk through strategies or listen to my concerns and answer my questions. And she still handles ordering my supplies and working with the health insurance company. Even though I have given permission to the insurance company for her to talk on my behalf (this is required since I am older than fifteen) she occasionally brings me in on the discussions so I understand how she talks through needs and coverage for the time I will need to handle this on my own. And even though I hear her in my head reminding me to bolus before I eat and to correct a trending high, she doesn't say these words out loud – most of the time.

I highly recommend that once your teenager has a good grasp on his/her insulin management, you let your teenager fail with their blood sugar every now and then. It teaches them how painfully difficult it is to deal with a high and low, causing them to stay more on top of their own care. This will ultimately help them be more successful long term.

CONTRIBUTING TO THE CURE

MICHELE

The one thing we all want is to find a cure that works, is affordable, and available to everyone. I mean honestly, is that too much to ask? I know it sounds cliché, but I recognize that understanding Jonathan's onset of type 1 diabetes (T1D) may be part of the solution for others. So, we are doing our part in two ways.

The first is by supporting companies and organizations involved in T1D solutions. We donate what we can to reputable charities who are involved in research we find promising. I find the studies interesting and like to read up on them so that I am aware of the opportunities that could be available to Jonathan. There are thousands of studies underway at any given time to test new technology, medications, and treatments. Some are in different phases of research and some are for patients in different phases of having T1D. The variance in some of them is so minimal that most people wouldn't even notice the difference. For example, using the same treatment but testing how to administer it differently. However, that difference could be the answer.

We also purchased stocks with the companies whose products Jonathan uses on a daily basis to manage his T1D and increase the number of shares as we can. In my mind, if we plan to use their products going forward, we should share in the successes of those companies.

The second thing we did was to enroll in a clinical trial. Most people don't realize that the majority of studies require the participant to be within twelve months of onset diagnosis. So by the time many of us get a sense of what we are doing and come up for air, we have missed the opportunity to help find a cure. I think part of the information packet we receive in the hospital should include sites that can be visited to learn about ongoing research and how to participate. A simple internet search for type 1 diabetes clinical trials will provide many websites and studies to review, along with the opportunity to request more information if interested in participating in them. There is everything from testing new technology to participating in scientific treatments.

We also went to the Breakthrough T1D website. Here we were able to answer a few questions that narrowed our qualifiers down to a list of potential clinical trials in which we were best suited to participate. (Interesting side note: this organization used to be called the Juvenile Diabetes Research Foundation. But as the demographics of those diagnosed changed to be almost equally children and adults, they changed their name to JDRF. On their website, they state the reason for this name change is to "remove the misconception that T1D is only a childhood disease and to acknowledge that nearly eighty-five percent of people living with T1D are over the age of eighteen...". They recently went through another brand change to Breakthrough T1D as they want to focus more on finding cures.)

Through our research, we found a two-year trial with the Joslin Diabetes Center and talked with our endocrinologist to get her thoughts. She is part-time in the clinic and part-time in the research lab, so we felt she would give us a good assessment as to whether we should participate and the possible risks associated with doing so. She reviewed the trial and gave us the green light as she thought it would have minimal negative side effects. After a few calls, a medical evaluation and the completion of several forms, Jonathan was accepted into the program. As he would be traveling to Boston once a month, we cleared the program with his school for the days he would miss and notified his teachers in advance so he could stay current with his work.

The study involved using Jonathan's own blood to see if the researchers could correct a problem with a group of immune regulatory cells that most people with T1D have, as well as reduce the immune system's attack on the remaining insulin-producing beta cells. Basically, if successful, the treatment would stop the destruction of the pancreas and allow Jonathan to remain in the honeymooning phase indefinitely. To me this was an important opportunity as I believe one of the issues with finding a cure is being able to repopulate the beta cells for individuals. Right now, the research studies that are close to finding a cure require the individual with T1D to take immunosuppressant drugs so as to not reject the donor beta cells. If we can determine how to stop the destruction of Jonathan's beta cells, then maybe when science is ready, they can take a person's own beta cells and clone them which would increase the success rate and negate the need for immunosuppressant drugs.

With every good research project there usually is a control group. For this study, two-thirds of the participants received their "corrected cells" back and one-third received their own cells back without any modifications. Because it is a double blinded trial, we won't know if Jonathan was part of the test or control group until after all the research is completed. But so far his testing seems to be producing stable results, which is really good news. Also, Jonathan's endocrinologist believes he is still honeymooning after two years given his minimal basal insulin needs.

He has been such an inspiration to me the entire time I have watched him go through this study. Not only in keeping up with his schoolwork, but also in participating in all the tests throughout the entire trial.

The first time we flew up to Boston it was in the summer. We spent five days enjoying the city because I wanted him to have other memories of Boston than just the research hospital. We walked everywhere and he barely bolused for any food because he stayed pretty low between the temperature and all the exercise. One evening he did run high because we ate and then didn't walk as much as we planned. His solution? Run up and down the twelve flights stairwell in our hotel. He was back in range for the remainder of the night.

After that trip we most often flew up to Boston on Sunday nights, spent Mondays at the study and then flew home in the evenings getting in around 2 am on Tuesday mornings – because he didn't like to miss his classes.

JONATHAN

My mom asked my doctor about clinical trials during our first follow-up appointment. She had read a lot about the scientific studies that were underway and the success that many of them were experiencing. My doctor, who is also a researcher, didn't recommend any of the studies she knew about because of my age and that I was relatively healthy.

My mom conducted weeks of research to learn about the different trials out there and which one would most benefit me without harming me. She found the one with the Joslin Diabetes Center and thought it was the best opportunity to save what was left of my pancreas and hopefully position me as a good candidate to clone my remaining beta cells to cure me. She walked me through what was going to be done and I said I would do it. She then shared the details with my doctor who felt it was the safest type of trial to participate in because it didn't involve donor cells.

Honestly, I was nervous about participating in the trial. But I trusted my mom and my doctor. So about five months after I was diagnosed, we flew to Boston. I listened to the doctors at the Joslin Diabetes Clinic as to what would happen over the next two years. While I hoped I received the "corrected cells" and that it would work for me, I realized I might only be part of the control group. I also had to admit to myself that the whole study could have no impact for me whatsoever. I decided that I would be doing my part to find a cure, even if it meant it may not lead to a cure for me.

Overall the appointments weren't that bad. Sometimes they were more of a checkup than anything else. The only part that was extremely painful was when they did the leukapheresis procedure.

For this procedure, I was hooked up to a machine that took the blood out of one arm, separated out the cells they needed for the treatment and then put the remaining blood back into my body – all in one process. Once they got everything set up and turned on the machine, it took a little more than four hours to complete. During that time, I experienced a sharp pain throughout my body that is hard to describe except to say I hope I never feel it again. My blood sugar hoovered around 270 mg/dL the entire time due to the immense pain. So not only was I experiencing the effects of the leukapheresis process, but I was also dealing with the headaches and body stress that usually accompany high blood sugar levels.

They put on a movie to help distract me. Between that and going to a "happy place" inside my head, I was able to complete the procedure. Afterwards, I bolused for half of the recommended amount of insulin because I knew from previous experience that the impact on my blood sugar from the pain would subside on its own. Then we walked around the neighborhood to level out my blood sugar before we ate lunch as I do not like to eat when I am running high. I am glad that we got that procedure out of the way early on in the trial and I only had to do it once. It took three additional visits for the researchers to put my cells back into my body. For the most part, those appointments were much easier. That process lasted about forty-five minutes each visit. We determined which arm worked the best for me and used that arm every time to minimize any discomfort.

The only other part of the trial that is somewhat uncomfortable is the glucose tolerance testing. This is where I drink a high carb protein shake (without bolusing) and then the researchers take blood from me every thirty minutes over a four hour span to measure how my body is responding to the glucose in my system. Again, dealing with the high blood sugar level is the worst part of the process. So far, my body has been able to bring my blood sugar down about 100 points on its own. I hope that is good news for me long-term. When each testing session is complete, I bolus insulin for the full amount my Personal Diabetes Manager (PDM) recommends based on my blood sugars. We also walk around for a while until my blood sugar stabilizes before eating. This is important to me because we usually are hopping on a plane later that evening and I want my blood sugar to be stable before I board the plane.

My mom asked if I would recommend participating in a clinical trial to others, or even if I would be willing to participate in another one given all I have experienced. I think if people feel comfortable and their doctors say it looks safe, they should do it because it is going to take all of us to cure this autoimmune disease.

As for me participating in another trial, I am open to it. It would depend on what was being researched and what I would need to do.

DIABETES DOES NOT DEFINE HIM

MICHELE

The most important thing I stress to Jonathan is that he has diabetes, but he is not diabetic. In other words, T1D doesn't define who he is. Defining yourself as a "diabetic" focuses on your limitations and allows others to create constraints for what they think you can and can't do.

Additionally, every conversation we have can't focus on diabetes and glucose levels. We had a strong relationship prior to him being diagnosed. We talked about anything and everything. That shouldn't change now that he has T1D.

Of course, it was difficult to avoid early in his diagnosis. For those of us with newly diagnosed teenagers, we have less time to help them understand what to do before we set them free as adults. Even though we needed to have many conversations focused on T1D during those first few months, I was cognizant that most of my interactions with him had become about diabetes. It had not only taken over our lives, but our conversations and our relationship as well.

I gave him the tools and knowledge to manage T1D on his own. He's been with me every step of the way and we have discussed the different bolus strategies in detail. Plus he understands how his T1D devices work. He is a young adult and I have to let him manage it on his own. Even if that means he rides higher than normal on some days or spikes toward 200 mg/dL because he is testing how a new food impacts him or he forgot to bolus for the meal.

Now I try to ensure I am asking him about his day, his schoolwork and his friends before I talk about T1D – even if I only want to share some exciting research news. Sometimes I choose to bring it up later when it makes more sense to insert it into that conversation. Trust me, as a type A mom, this isn't easy. In my mind, I want to talk about it and move on. There, I said it. We resolved it. We don't have to think about it (until it happens again). But that is not how my boy works. It is not how Jonathan processes information and me pushing it into the situation often means that I have to bring it up again when he is ready to hear what I want to share. So I learned to be ready for when he wants to listen.

Same is true for texting. I don't want every text to be about T1D because I don't want him to start ignoring them. While we used texting as our primary channel for T1D communication during high school, I avoid using it for anything T1D now.

It may not seem like it at first, but it does get easier. Believe me when I tell you things become routine. If you do the heavy lifting early on after being diagnosed and learn how your teenager's body responds to food and insulin, you will get the hang of how to bolus, how to correct highs and lows, and how to use the available technology. You will swag the carb count and be pretty close, even when you are eating out at a new restaurant. You will successfully determine how to bolus for the special occasion foods and how to catch the lows without taking a rollercoaster ride.

The lingo begins to roll off your tongue and find its way into everyday conversations without you even realizing it. The other day Jonathan and I were walking and he was talking to me about an issue he was having with higher-than-desired glucose levels and how he planned to adjust his bolusing approach. We passed an older couple walking who gave us an odd look. It was only then that I realized Jonathan was nonchalantly talking about "being high" and here I was, his mother, just listening. They must have assumed he was talking about recreational drugs vs T1D. Oh well.

You'll read through online posts and recognize you went through the same situation and came out safely on the other side. You'll be able to share with confidence what worked in your situations and encourage others so they learn to manage T1D successfully. The diabetic memes make sense and even become funny in an understanding sort of way.

When Jonathan's first Diaversary (anniversary of his diagnosis day) rolled around on the calendar, I paused and gave thanks for how far we have come on our journey. We have fought the initial battles thrown at us by this autoimmune disease with eyes wide open and have built the attack plans Jonathan uses daily. Throughout all the decisions, when I had a choice to make, it became very clear to me that I will always choose Jonathan. We will use the information that is out there and Jonathan's doctors as guidance for us. But when it comes down to it, I choose to go with what Jonathan wants to do in his T1D management.

My son has type 1 diabetes. He is not a type 1 diabetic. It may seem like something small, but it really is a mindset.

Jonathan is a college student,
He is a drummer,
He is a gamer,
He is a taekwondo instructor ... who has T1D.
But not the other way around.

Jonathan is a son,
He is a brother,
He is a friend ... who has T1D.

And someday...
Jonathan may be allowed to be an astronaut.

JONATHAN

One decision can change your entire life forever. I choose to be an active, healthy individual who happens to have T1D.

This decision alone has brought so many benefits to my life. I do everything I can to make my body as healthy as possible so I don't have to worry about the complications of T1D and so T1D doesn't dominate my daily life. I also have made the decision to help others. To advocate for research, better medical coverage, and talk openly about the decisions I make and how those same decisions can provide new paths for others who are willing to make them.

Even if the gym is not your thing, you can be active and healthier in other ways. It's making the decision to take a walk, try a new activity or eat better than the day before.

Our lives are full of decisions each day, each moment. That next decision you make can change your life and put you on a path to achieving a happier and healthier future.

T1D to me has a new meaning in my life. "Takes 1 Decision" is my mantra and the message I want to spread. That even if life throws you a curveball or things don't go as you have planned, it's the choices you make afterward that define who you are and how beneficial your life will be.

TYPE 1, YEAR ONE TAKEAWAYS

Healthy T1D Management Essentials

- ☐ Educate yourself on T1D, current technology and available treatment options, so you can advocate for proper care and accommodations
- ☐ Determine your personal insulin-to-carb ratios, basal levels, and correction factors
- ☐ Wear a continuous glucose monitor (CGM) and program it with tight alerts to mitigate highs and lows before they become dangerous
- ☐ Stay active to help your body maintain its insulin sensitivity
- ☐ Learn how your body responds to daily factors that impact glucose levels
- ☐ Hydration is important for accurate CGM numbers and insulin movement in the body
- ☐ Make small adjustments and don't be afraid of the trial and error process
- ☐ Understand how to determine the carbohydrates, fat and protein in your food so you can bolus correctly

Strategies to Minimize the Rollercoaster Effect

- ☐ Start simple and add complexity to your diet as you learn how your body responds to food and insulin
- ☐ Target no more than 30-40 complex carbs per meal
- ☐ Learn when your body needs a pre-, extended, or temporary bolus
- ☐ Determine when correction boluses are needed to get your glucose back into a healthy range
- ☐ Develop an insulin strategy when eating out, traveling and being active

Other Recommendations

- ☐ Recognize signs of mental struggles (grief, burnout, anxiety, etc.) and find professional help to work through them
- ☐ Join in-person and online support group to connect with other T1D Warriors
- ☐ Use monthly subscription services and automatic refills for your preferred foods, glucose solutions, and prescriptions
- ☐ Request accommodations for school and work as needed
- ☐ Look into apps and other technology that can help you with better diabetes management
- ☐ Take advantage of all the benefits your health insurance provides
- ☐ Create an organized space for your T1D supplies

- ❏ Consider testing others in your family for the T1D genetic markers
- ❏ Be flexible and give yourself grace

RESOURCES

Books
- Bright Spots and Landmines by Adam Brown
- Dr. Bernstein's Diabetes Solution by Richard K. Bernstein, MD
- On Grief and Grieving by Elisabeth Kubler-Ross and David Kessler
- Sugar Surfing by Dr. Ponder
- Think like a Pancreas by Gary Scheiner

Facebook Pages
- All Day I Dream About Food
- Bold with Insulin
- Juicebox Podcast: Type 1 Diabetes
- Wholesome Yum – Easy Healthy Recipes

Podcasts
- Juicebox Podcast

Websites
- American Diabetes Association: www.diabetes.org/diabetes/type-1
- Beyond Type 1: www.beyondtype1.org
- Breakthrough T1D: www.breakthroughT1D.org
- Dexcom: www.dexcom.com/en-us
- Diabetic Athletic: www.diabeticathletic.com/homepage
- Diabetes Mall: www.diabetesnet.com
- DiaTribe: www.DiaTribe.org
- Omnipod: www.omnipod.com
- The Diabetes Link: www.thediabeteslink.org
- T1D Mod Squad: www.t1dmodsquad.org

ACKNOWLEDGMENTS

Special thanks to my friends and family for their support and valuable feedback while writing this book. Thank you, Jonathan, for your valuable input and openness.

If you have found this book valuable, please post a review or rating on the website where you bought it so that the website's algorithm will make the book visible to others. Your decision may help someone else achieve better T1D management.

AUTHOR BIO

Michele Segura is an accomplished strategist and communications professional with leadership experience in the financial, healthcare, energy and insurance industries. She chooses to be a lifelong learner and has built her career on accepting new opportunities that continue to stretch and challenge her. Michele has dedicated her life, skills and knowledge to helping others, whether on the job or through volunteering with non-profit and education-based organizations. Fueled by a fresh cup of coffee, she thrives on tackling problems and finding solutions that address needs, improve processes, and create better user experiences.

Connect with the author: Takes1Decision@gvtc.com

Made in the USA
Monee, IL
14 January 2025